James Levi

The Seventh Man

The Story of the Men from the Samaritan Woman's Life

James Levi, Ph.D.

ISBN: 978-1-7344551-2-0

Cover design: Lifexcel Leadership Series Publication

Published by: Lifexcel Leadership Series Publication,
P.O Box 953 Huntsville, Texas 77342

For Worldwide Distribution, Printed in the U.S.A.

1 2 3 4 5 6 /18 17 16 15

For more information please contact: Lifexcel Leadership Series Publishing at lifexcelleadershipseries@gmail.com

DEDICATION

To Namrata, our second daughter and the delight of your mom's and my life. Your spirit, your focus, and your love make me smell your freshly baked cheese jalapeño bread every day.

James Levi

CONTENTS

Acknowledgments

Introduction

1   Water Jar   13

2   Recognition to Relationship   31

3   Denying to Giving   67

4   Religion to Worship   107

5   Prophet to Messiah   127

6   Man to Husband   143

7   Ahni   155

8   Well to Spring   181

9   The Seventh Man   191

ACKNOWLEDGMENTS

I want to extend a special thank you to all my spiritual mentors and companions who have walked the dark and lonely path with me. I am grateful to many who accompanied me on my journey as a thirsty traveler and refreshed my life with "Living Water." I am also grateful to Dr. Dale Kietzman, who blessed me beyond measure with his compassionate and encouraging life example.

James Levi

Now Jesus learned that the Pharisees had heard that he was gaining and baptizing more disciples than John — although in fact it was not Jesus who baptized, but his disciples. So, he left Judea and went back once more to Galilee.

Now he had to go through Samaria. So, he came to a town in Samaria called Sychar, near the plot of ground Jacob had given to his son Joseph. Jacob's well was there, and Jesus, tired as he was from the journey, sat down by the well. It was about noon.

When a Samaritan woman came to draw water, Jesus said to her, "Will you give me a drink?" (His disciples had gone into the town to buy food.)

The Samaritan woman said to him, "You are a Jew, and I am a Samaritan woman. How can you ask me for a drink?" (For Jews do not associate with Samaritans.)

Jesus answered her, "If you knew the gift of God and who it is that asks you for a drink, you would have asked him, and he would have given you living water."

"Sir," the woman said, "you have nothing to draw with, and the well is deep. Where can you get this living water? Are you greater than our father Jacob, who gave us the well and drank from it himself, as did also his sons and his livestock?"

Jesus answered, "Everyone who drinks this water will be thirsty again, but whoever drinks the water I give them will never thirst. Indeed, the water I give them will become in them a spring of water welling up to eternal life."

The woman said to him, "Sir, give me this water so that I won't get thirsty and have to keep coming here to draw water."

He told her, "Go, call your husband and come back."

"I have no husband," she replied.

Jesus said to her, "You are right when you say you have no husband. The fact is, you have had five husbands, and the man you now have is not your husband. What you have just said is quite true."

"Sir," the woman said, "I can see that you are a prophet. Our ancestors worshiped on this mountain, but you Jews claim that the place where we must worship is in Jerusalem."

"Woman," Jesus replied, "believe me, a time is coming when you will worship the Father neither on this mountain nor in Jerusalem. You Samaritans worship what you do not know; we worship what we do know, for salvation is from the Jews. Yet a time is coming and has

now come when the true worshipers will worship the Father in the Spirit and in truth, for they are the kind of worshipers the Father seeks. God is spirit, and his worshipers must worship in the Spirit and in truth."

The woman said, "I know that Messiah" (called Christ) is coming. When he comes, he will explain everything to us."

Then Jesus declared, "I, the one speaking to you — I am he."

Just then his disciples returned and were surprised to find him talking with a woman. But no one asked, "What do you want?" or "Why are you talking with her?"

Then, leaving her water jar, the woman went back to the town and said to the people, "Come, see a man who told me everything I ever did. Could this be the Messiah?" They came out of the town and made their way toward him.

Meanwhile, his disciples urged him, "Rabbi, eat something."

But he said to them, "I have food to eat that you know nothing about."

Then his disciples said to each other, "Could someone have brought him food?"

"My food," said Jesus "is to do the will of him who sent me and to finish his work. Don't you have a saying, 'It's still four months until harvest?' I tell you, open your eyes and look at the fields! They are ripe for harvest. Even now the one who reaps draws a wage and harvests a crop for eternal life so that the sower and the reaper may be glad together. Thus the saying 'One sows and another reaps' is true. I sent you to reap what you have not worked for. Others have done the hard work, and you have reaped the benefits of their labor."

Many of the Samaritans from that town believed in him because of the woman's testimony, "He told me everything I ever did." So when the Samaritans came to him, they urged him to stay with them, and he stayed two days. And because of his words, many more became believers.

They said to the woman, "We no longer believe just because of what you said; now we have heard for ourselves, and we know that this man really is the Savior of the world" (John 4:1-42).

Introduction

Las Vegas!

We left the city and made our way onto the highway. It was past noon. The scorching sun of the Nevada desert was merciless, and the heat could melt our dashboard. It was Saturday, and the road was empty, so my friend Jay put the pedal to the metal and kept it there. Both of us were seminarians and ministers (at different churches), and we wanted to get back to Los Angeles before nightfall, in time for our Sunday morning services. We didn't want to be late and certainly didn't want to let our congregations know where we had been hiding the last few nights!

We had decided to take a break from our theology books, ancient language studies, and late nights of researching at the library to run off to a city that people say never sleeps. We found it to be true to its name. Upon arrival, we were immediately immersed in its glamour, glimmer, and glut. It was my first visit, and Jay made sure that I didn't miss anything (with the refrain, "What happens in Vegas stays in Vegas"). We walked through the streets, laughed with the crowd, enjoyed food truck treats, bought souvenirs, and met a few people who were there to play, pay, and prey (and, for some, "pray" that the night wouldn't end). The bright lights illuminated the city, and the loud music drowned out any other noise. All the laughter and action made it almost impossible for anyone to be alone.

Still tired from our journey, we made our way to a restaurant. I don't know why we chose that place, but I still remember amazing live music playing in the background. We were in the middle of eating our meal when we noticed her.

She was the kind of woman you couldn't help by notice, she wore her wealth — and the little she wore spoke of it loudly. She was attractive, but she also wore her age. She staggered a bit as she walked and took the seat right next to us. Without any formal introduction, she just started pouring her heart out to us. Within moments, she was in tears as she shared her anguish with us.

"This is not the life I ever signed up for…all these men ever want is to use me, cheat on me and in the end make me feel abused. I don't believe in this institution called marriage anymore…I am tired!"

Jay and I looked at each other wide-eyed, asking silently: "How in the world could she know that we were pastors?" As she sobbed, her words were hard to understand, but her pain was clear, and we felt it deeply. Then, just as suddenly as she had walked in and sat down beside us, the woman stood up and walked out. It was surreal; one moment we were hearing her cry, feeling her pain, and listening to her story — and the next moment she was gone! But she left behind the memory of her words of pain, her tears, and her feelings of anger against herself, men, and maybe her whole world. The music behind us got louder as her steps faded further and further away. Neither Jay nor I had the chance to say a word to her, but we had both soaked in the experience of that moment. Silently, we watched the band clearing the stage and packing up their equipment. I don't remember how long we stayed, but eventually we returned to our hotel rooms to sleep.

When we woke up the next day, it was almost midday. We grabbed some breakfast to go and hit the road heading home. Usually Jay and I spoke non-stop when we traveled together. But this time we hardly said anything.

As we drove along an empty highway, we suddenly saw something strange coming up immediately ahead of us. As if out of nowhere, a lone traveler appeared, walking on the side of the deserted road. Jay and I glanced at each other quickly as our car whizzed past him. I looked back trying to get a glimpse of the traveler's face. I couldn't see him very well, but somehow, I sensed this was a man on assignment. I was thrown slightly forward in my passenger seat. I was lost in the moment and Jay had brought the car to an abrupt stop. He said, "Hey, let's give him a ride."

What? Immediately my mind started racing and fear started rising. Surely it was not safe to invite a stranger into our car! What if he was armed? Jay didn't ask for my permission and he seemed sure of what he was doing. The man kept on walking. A minute later he was next to our idling car. I slowly rolled down my window, and Jay smiled as he invited him to get in. The man accepted the offer and quietly slipped into the back seat, placing his backpack right next to him and settling in. I was still quite nervous. I tried to subtly snatch a look at him in my side view mirror (I needed to remember his face in case something went wrong). What I saw was the ordinary face of a man, tired from a long journey. But he looked remarkably peaceful, as tired as he was. Jay struck up a conversation with the stranger. His name was Ahni. He was headed to a nearby town to find work. He spoke in an uncommonly soft tone, slowly, gently, calmly. The remainder of the trip lasted less than an hour and was mostly quiet. We soon reached Ahni's stop, but before he got out Jay gave him some money to buy himself a meal, which Ahni gladly accepted. As we drove back onto the highway, I looked back to get one last glimpse of him, and there he was, once again walking on the side of the road with those legs. But a moment later, something strange happened: Ahni disappeared into thin air! I grabbed Jay's hand and cried out about what I had just seen. He swiftly pulled the car over to side of the road and we both looked back in total amazement. We continued staring at the road behind us and trembled with fear, shock, and confusion about Ahni's mysterious disappearance. After a few moments, our eyes spotted something that he had left behind on the back seat; it looked somewhat like a book, but it didn't appear to be an ordinary book. The pages were tied together by what looked like leather straps from an ancient and historic time, and the item seemed sacred in some way. It looked like it had been treasured for a long time, and the pages had faded to a pale yellow, indicating that it had weathered a few rough seasons over the years. My hands shook as I went to pick it up…it was a bit heavy with a few loose pages that tore slightly as I lifted it up. I carefully opened it and was surprised to see that the text was written in a form of ancient script that I, as a seminarian, had been studying. I could barely contain my excitement as Jay turned off the engine and waited impatiently as I explored the first page, my mouth wide open in awe. He listened intently as I read the words of the text out loud.

"One normal sluggish afternoon, one unnamed, unrighteous, unaccepted woman from an unholy town called Sychar in Samaria did a very unusual thing, quite unlike her."

Something mystical unfolded as I read from the pages of the book, unlike anything I'd experienced before. I wasn't simply reading words on a page; I was reading words that were transformed into what I can only describe as "living water," I told Jay. Even Jay felt it, confirming that every time I spoke a word from the book, it seemed like we were no longer on a deserted highway. We now understood, deeply and profoundly, that the calm-spirited and peaceful stranger that we had just invited into our car was no ordinary man at all, and the book that he left behind was no ordinary book.

We were received in Los Angeles by a beautifully lit skyline just as the bright orange-yellow sun was going down. We had so many questions, but the one that burdened us the most was this: Had Ahni mistakenly forgotten his precious book, or had he left it behind with us for a much bigger purpose? As I continued to read out loud, it became increasingly clear: this book was meant to be read by more than just the two of us sitting in the car that afternoon; it was a book to be revealed to the world. Therefore, on behalf of our mysterious stranger and friend Ahni, I invite you to embark on a life-transforming journey that began in an ancient time and a faraway land.

James Levi

Chapter 1

Water Jar

Then, leaving her water jar, the woman [who had five husbands, and the man she now has is not her husband] *went back to the town and said to the people, "…could this be the Messiah?"* (John 4:28-29).

The Unnamed Woman

One normal sluggish afternoon, one unnamed, unrighteous, unaccepted woman from an unholy town called Sychar in Samaria did a very unusual thing, quite unlike her. Her behavior shocked everyone who knew her. That day she returned to the village empty-handed! She returned to town shouting about a man she met at the well, and she was so excited about what the man told her that she left her precious personal water jar behind. She had never done that before and probably had never even imagined doing so. Whenever she went to the well, the water jar went with her, and whenever she returned, it remained with her. (Some today might find it humorous to see the parallel to Mary of the "little lamb" fame. Remember the nursery rhyme, "And everywhere that Mary went the lamb was sure to go"? Well, everywhere this Samaritan woman went, the water jar was sure to go!)

In the story from the ancient text, even though the town's name is mentioned, the woman's name is not. Was it a deliberate omission because her name didn't mean anything important or have any significance? Was it that she had been forgotten amid the everyday activities of the town and the busyness of its people?

Walking to Jacob's well with her water jar could symbolize freedom from everything that was tying her down, her history of broken relationships, everything that tried to break her inner self and her very spirit. It became a very personal, solitary time for her; walking away from town and carrying her water jar gave her a purpose to live for and a time that she looked forward to every day. This was something she was good at doing. The time alone gave her a sense of her own identity. At the well she sought and claimed her sacred, personal space, a private place where she enjoyed very precious moments, connecting with her inner world and detaching from her outside world. Walking to the well was a spiritual experience, not solely physical — it was a holy time for her.

Summer heat didn't bother her, the rain didn't stop her, and even cold winter days didn't thwart her mission; she was at Jacob's well every noontime with her water jar. The time at the well allowed her once again to dream of a life that she had imagined as a young, innocent girl walking with her mother, clasping her strong hand. Those moments with her mother were powerful because she spoke to her about how beautifully and wonderfully she was created by God to be used for his glory and how much God loved her. Her mother's words, trusted words, were an oasis during her formative years. There was no fear, no shame, and no guilt back then, only the warmth of her mother's unconditional love enveloped every step as they walked together.

Now, whenever she followed that path toward the well, those memories flooded her mind and spirit. She once again heard her mother's voice saying: "Your life circumstances do not define you, but the promises of the Almighty do, the One, who said that you are highly favored and blessed by him." Walking on the path to the well filled her heart with peace and strength and joy that she knew surpassed her human understanding and life circumstances.

But then, as they say, "life happened," and her dreams came tumbling down, crushed under the mighty waves of pain and deceit, lost in the reality of a hard life. An outside force tried to crush her inside; innocence was snatched away, and her life broke into a thousand pieces. When she tried to pick up the shattered remains, she was belittled, abused, ignored, and cast aside.

Now the only thing she could do was remember those dreams as often as she could, attempt to keep them alive at least in her memory, and make some peace with herself as she walked the lonely path that led to the well, the water jar in her arms. During those walks to the well, first, tears fell, and then she would miraculously be lifted into the presence of the Almighty, filled with the peace that only comes from above, just as her mother described it. In those moments, she once again experienced life, joy, and strength — deaf to all the other voices that accused her of defeat, failure, and evil. It was at that moment she could feel in her spirit that "the weapons of damage and insult formed against her would not prosper." She understood that she was not forgotten or lost, even though life didn't make sense. There was someone bigger than her biggest messes.

At the well she could feel refreshed within her soul with the water from a fountain that springs forth from within — even if only for a moment.

This lonely noontime at the well with the water jar allowed her to truly live life as she escaped the condemning eyes and gossiping lips of her people in her village. As they tried to eject her from society, she sought to fight their rejection with isolation. Thus, she looked forward to this personal time with her water jar, the time when she could be free and not judged.

The water jar was more than just a container that carried a life-giving resource; it had become her freedom from harassment and shame. That's why she held on to it so tightly and protected it so carefully. It offered solace in that comforting place at the well; it gave her hope and strength to fight back and provided safety by helping her find a way to cope with her internal turmoil, her dark world, her fears, her emotions, and the unknowns of life.

The jar and what it represented slowly gave her a new self — someone very different from the self she didn't like and was running away from, just as she ran from her own people. The walk with the jar allowed her to hide from others as well as from herself; she didn't have to deal with people nor with her true self. She lived a new life at the well. Every day she looked forward to this time, and nothing would keep her from it. As long as she had this time at the well, if she had the jar by her side, she didn't need anything else or anyone else. She would fight to stop and block anyone from ever taking away her water jar — and thereby her time, her sacred space, and her new identity. The jar represented her world, her life, and her refuge.

People who tried to snatch it failed; those who were bold and approached her often experienced a harsh pushback that exposed her ugly side. Some said, "We don't know who she has become. Did she just become someone else, or was she always like this? Who would ever be like this?"

Let it Go

But this afternoon, near Jacob's well, something strange happened that many would call nothing short of a miracle. Speaking with the man stirred within her something so profound that it turned her world inside out. She had let go of her water jar for the very first time! Or…did she let go of herself?

Walking away from the well without her water jar released a whole new person. A simple meeting with a man who had asked for a drink from her water jar left *her* never drinking from her old self anymore. It was like a new hope birthing forth for a tree. Once this tree was cut down, but now it was sprouting again. Those with new shoots that will not fail. Its roots had for some time had grown old in the ground and its stump had died in the soil yet like at the scent of water it did bud and put forth shoots like a plant (Job 14: 7-9), this woman was becoming new once again. The hardened soil was cracked open and a new soul from the inside walked out. Nothing was impossible now, and nothing was going to be the same.

Something deep within her was touched and filled, and out of it sprung forth newness, hope, beauty, and excitement. She returned to town totally different from the way she had left. Something had drastically changed in her life, something that no one in her village could have caused. Neither she nor her people had imagined this day ever coming. The world around her had written her off, and her life was falling apart, yet it was in that weak, fragile moment that something moved within her. This new life within her was greater than the one she was living on the outside!

It had not been easy for her to let go of the water jar, but she did.

Her plan for the day suddenly and abruptly came to a halt when the man asked her for a drink — that divine moment. He spoke gently, unhurriedly, and softly within her, peeling the hidden, hardened, intimate, shamed layers one at a time. Though she had a daily routine that she followed strictly, she never wanted anything to interfere with her visits to the well or with her water jar. In fact, she would fight with every ounce of her strength to adhere to her precise plan, because the familiar routine calmed her fears, gave her control, and made her feel in charge of her life. But today was different; today she was unafraid to let go of the water jar. She was excited to run back to the village and share the good news with everyone. For the first time in her life, she was willing to leave the water jar behind and move into a new and hopeful future. All this happened because she encountered someone at the well. Someone had met her in both an extraordinary and intimate way. The man had waited to meet with her and showed respect for her as she had never experienced in her adult life. He treated her in a way that she had never known before and spoke to her as no one else ever had. He not only listened to her, but he also *heard* her. He touched her inner being gently and honorably. With his words, he spoke to her very soul and to her fears. He breathed comfort to her tired spirit and gave a peaceful rest that changed everything for her. She became *her* truest self. She was *born again.*

Run!

What followed the meeting with the man was very unusual — the unnamed woman ran! She ran to her village without her water jar, abandoning it at the well. For the first time, she felt fully complete without it, unashamed of herself, and determined not to obscure her scarred life with the jar anymore.

Her openness of who she was and being vulnerable of all the mistakes that she had ever made in her life surprised the people. Yet she stood there unashamed. Once being transparent about herself before the man at the well made her to totally own her marred life without fear and disgrace. This touched the chord of the villagers. Never had they seen such honesty and courage and gentleness all flowing together from this woman. They were instantly glued to who she had become.

Now she returned to the well, but not alone. This time, there was a crowd behind her; people from her village were following her to see the person she had spoken about: the man who had changed her. Amazingly, rather than hiding and trying to escape the crowd in Sychar, she was leading them! For the very first time, this "unrighteous outcast" who usually kept to herself now had a crowd following her.

What? A crowd following this unnamed woman with a tainted past? It was unheard of! Yet not only did the people want to go where she was leading them and experience what she said she had experienced, they totally believed her! They had witnessed a mystery unfold right in front of their eyes; a transformation in a woman that was nothing less than a wonder in itself. The whole village was now interested in someone they had always disregarded. The whole village was drawn to what compelled her.

First, they came one by one and looked at this strange outsider waiting at the well. He was a rabbi, a teacher — a Jew! — one with whom they would never mingle. They beheld him; they heard him, *really* heard him. They wanted more and more of him. Then came a strange request from the crowd: "We want to hear more from you, we want to drink more of your living water; we are thirsty. We want you to come home with us!"

What?

Now, this was a very unusual request coming from the village of Sychar. They rarely allowed outsiders onto their turf, but on this day at the well, they wanted this man to come to their village, be their guest, and stay in their homes. Would he say no — denying their offer was expected since he was a Jew and Jews did not associate with Samaritans — or would he accept? What would his people think? Did he have something to say to both groups and perhaps to all humanity? To everyone's surprise, the rabbi willingly agreed and spent two days in Sychar. This stranger, the Jewish teacher, agreed to stay with the unholy Samaritans! It was a new chapter in history; his action was insane to many, and blasphemous to others.

Strong Men from Sychar

As this story was unfolding in front of Jacob's well, there was something mystical happening within the hearts of some of the townspeople. Something was stirring inside and breaking within a few of the "rough dudes" of Sychar. It was a strange display of courage, tenderness, pain, and relief.

As the whole village approached the well, one man's gaze slowly moved from the teacher to the water jar that had been abandoned there. He felt a pull towards it. He moved closer, drawn to the object just as his spiritual father, Moses, was once attracted to the burning bush. The water jar, oddly, kindled a fire within this Sychar man; he was burning yet he was not consumed.

The jar had a story to tell, an odd tale connected to this man's life, his past, and something he had pushed away for a very long time. It had been a closed chapter. He recognized this water jar as representing something significant in his life: a powerful link to his past and a connection to a person from his earlier years. He thought it was strange because he had never seen that jar left alone or abandoned, and it stirred up curious feelings within him. Today he stood by the well, overwhelmed by the sight of the jar and lost in a moment of deep emotion. He recalled the story associated with the jar and memories started flooding his mind. Suddenly, without warning, warm tears rolled down his cheeks. Yes, something shook violently deep inside the spirit of this man from Sychar. From his eyes, once dry as his heart, wet tears fell. He was being watered again.

Men from Sychar didn't cry! They were taught to be tough, to "man up," and never exhibit their weakness in the open. They believed that only frail women and children cried, not proud men from Sychar. But today, this particular man, felt raw and broken. Yet, at the same time, he realized he was experiencing something sacred.

Suddenly, there was a hubbub at the well, and a few people started walking slowly to where the weeping man stood. They also felt a strong draw toward the water jar and assumed that same posture. One by one they all moved closer, inching toward the jar with fear and caution. They were confused, yet moved by what they were seeing, experiencing, and mystically surrendering to.

What was going on?

What was the power behind this ordinary water jar? How could a jar create such an extraordinary scenario in this remote place?

*****

This sacred moment and the scene at the well left many speechless. They were in awe at the sight of this mysterious group of powerful men. This was unannounced, unintentional, and overpowering. Each participant was caught off guard and outside of their comfort zone by the jar's effect on them. Could there be a common thread running through their stories, their histories, and their lives, connecting them uniquely?

I, Ahni, feeling the same emotion, counted, and there were a total of five men standing in silence with tears streaming down their faces while their eyes were fixed on the water jar at the well. They were shaking and trembling, losing all control yet unashamed, and maybe for the very first time letting go of something they had been holding onto for a very long time. Walls of pride, veils of fear, clouds of anger, and the pain of failure were all ripped open and exposed, vulnerable, and standing naked to their past and life. For so long they had been running from reality, hiding from the world around them and tired. But now they were willing to own their mistakes and assume the risk of being helpless. As individuals, a community of broken men, they stood...together.

How could an ordinary left-behind jar ignite such a fire and create such an emotional rousing in such tough men? What is this mysterious experience they were sharing but couldn't explain?

This all began with a change in the unnamed woman at the well but exploded into a healing for so many more. The process that started at the well one afternoon with a humble request, "I thirst," not only affected the town of Sychar but has set millions of profoundly thirsty people free throughout the ages from places far and wide. It still has the power to heal. To this day, the story that began with a woman followed by five men (six including me, Ahni) is still calling out, to anyone who is feeling the thirst to live their life to the fullest.

The clear voice still heard crying from the old, rugged, wooden cross rings in life's wilderness, calling out, "I thirst! Father, forgive them!" There is a place where the lost are found, broken ones are healed, and outcasts are restored with a new purpose. There is the man who promises that *the water He gives will become in us "a spring of water welling up to eternal life."*

*****

I invite you to walk with me through the following pages as I take the pleasure of introducing these men from Sychar. I came to know each of them through the sage named Ahni, the man from the past who left a treasure for us. Reading his words and getting to know these men has changed my life forever. There will be more about Ahni in a later chapter, but before that meet each of the men he describes, know their stories and learn about their mystical connection to the water jar. You will also meet the owner of the water jar and the reason why she left it at the well. Finally, you will meet the man, the "Seventh Man," she met at the well. This encounter will allow each of us to meet our true selves and, if we are honest, will take us deep into the places where we may not have the strength to travel, but where his presence will go with us.

Today is the day for anyone to "Come, see a man…"

James Levi

The Seventh Man

Chapter 2

Recognition to Relationship

He told her, "Go, call your husband and come back." "I have no husband," she replied. Jesus said to her, "You are right when you say you have no husband. The fact is, you have had five husbands, and the man you now have is not your husband. What you have just said is quite true." (John 4:17-18)

Aleph, the First Husband

The people of Sychar remembered it in detail from the beginning, as it was the talk of the town. They all said that it was a beautiful courtship that led to two families in the same village uniting in holy matrimony. People were glad, women were excited to wear new dresses, children were looking forward to the fun, and everyone was happy for the couple. Some referred to them as the perfect couple; they complemented each other well. Both were ambitious and driven and, according to many, they were the couple who would "make things happen."

The wedding was beautiful, with a reception held under the evening sky that was heavy with stars and unusually bright, overlooking the Mediterranean Sea. It was followed by a lavish honeymoon. Everything was going well, or at least it seemed to be, until something changed not long after the trip. The difference was noticeable to those who knew the couple well. The couple didn't appear to appreciate and admire each other the way they did when they were courting. Did something happen in the initial days of their marriage? What went wrong? Why did the newness wear off? None of the town gossips had any good stories to tell; at least none that would sell in these Eastern markets.

Gone were the days of the past when the would-be bride had only praise for the incredible man she had chosen. Aleph had completed his studies at the Samaritan Law College with an outstanding academic track record, followed by an impressive internship at the town's famous Mordecai Cultural and Religious Center. He worked with some influential policymakers, and now he was ready to take on the world. With clear goals in mind, he was embarking on his future as a career politician. His eyes were set on becoming the next mayor of Sychar, where he would be able to change how people lived. He knew how to promote himself and make promises to connect to the hearts of his constituency. Among many such promises, one was to build a healthy relationship with the neighboring Jews (who had been marginalized from the Sychar community for quite a long time). Another promise of his campaign manifesto was to help the women of the town who were struggling with problems involving safe drinking water. It looked like he had all the answers to the community's difficulties, yet he didn't know the answers to the questions he was facing in his own personal life.

Meanwhile, his wife daydreamed of sharing in his success and being in the media spotlight, surrounded by fans. Admiration from the crowd and appreciation from people were what she longed for. She had always dreamed of being the center of attention, and here was an opportunity to become the first lady of the town. But her dream didn't last long after the marriage began. Little did she know that the man she married was not the man she thought she knew so well. According to her, he became a different man altogether — or maybe she had simply never known who he really was? As the weeks went by, and then the months, he wanted nothing to do with her, other than to use her for his own advantage to canvas villagers for votes. Many nights she tried to start a conversation with her husband, but he always turned away from her coldly. Unless the topic was about him or his plans and his drive to reach the top political spheres, there was silence, and abrupt ends to conversations. For him, she was not a priority, only a means to his end goal, which was to become famous and popular, reaching the mayoral office, and becoming the Savior of Sychar and Samaria, and to all his world. In other words, it was all about him.

The change in their relationship hit her hard and left her depressed. She felt marginalized and like she was nothing more than a piece of furniture to be moved around in their home. When her husband wanted to host parties to please his constituency and to show off to his people that he was an ideal family man, he would ask her to dress up and appear cheerful, caring, and as an overall appealing Samaritan wife. That would win the voters' hearts and minds. In short order, this artificial life and the harsh reality that he had a selfish and narcissistic personality were painful truths for her to bear. It led her to become detached, dejected, and hurtful. She was angry with him and she would not put up with his demands. She was frustrated that he never truly accepted her or acknowledged her needs. She felt so forgotten, ignored, and uncared for that she came to feel there was no meaning and no purpose to her life.

When she could bear it no more, she sought help, first from the elders of the Sychar village council. When she received no positive response from them, she sought help from the religious healers. There also she found no answers. Some said her troubles were due to a bad omen or a strange star that appeared in the east some time ago. According to them, that was the possible reason for her failed marriage.

She tried to fashion happiness out of her despair. She attempted to make friends in the village, but people simply ignored her and started saying negative things about her. Some people bluntly accused her of being the reason for her husband's failure to be nominated for political office and failing to achieve his dreams. Once again, her hopes for having a quality life were dashed. She was broken and didn't want to have anything to do with anything or anybody. She decided to avoid the gossips of the town and go alone to the well during the noon hour and fill the water jar all by herself.

Although at first it was a lonely and long walk, she soon discovered that it was not that difficult, and she could tolerate it. It was certainly easier than facing the hurtful stories and rude remarks from the women, who always found a reason to put her down in an attempt to break her spirit.

In time, she found herself enjoying this time of walking to the well all by herself. She could express her feelings of rejection and loneliness out loud. She didn't have to care about what people thought or how they judged her. It was therapeutic and eased some of the pain. Her attachment to the walks with her water jar had grown to the point where she would organize her plans for the day early in the morning, to make sure that she would have time to savor her noontime walk to the well. She would tuck all her thoughts inside her until she was on the dusty road, and then she would share everything in her heart and in her mind with her friend and only support — the water jar. It might not have seemed to make sense to the outside world, but to the unnamed woman it made perfect sense. On those walks to the well, Jacob's well, her inner world and all her senses came alive.

Her husband began to feel rejected and suspicious, even accusing her of having an affair because she was spending so much time away from home. She was no longer available to help him organize political meetings or take care of his election campaigning. Every time he requested her assistance, she was too busy going to the well, alone and always carrying her water jar. They even fought over the water jar but she held her ground; she would not give up her appointment at the well.

In the end, they decided to end their marriage. It was heartbreaking news in the small village of Sychar; everyone who knew the couple had thought they were the perfect match. No one thought this celebrity couple would split in such a sad way, or that their marriage would end in such tragedy. Although they lost each other, she kept the water jar.

Throughout the time of dissolution, the husband had never inquired what was wrong with her or why she was behaving the way she did. He never stopped his fierce political campaigning long enough to care.

The treatment she endured in her marriage broke her. She would never again trust another man because, in her mind, every man just wanted to use her. She thought that all men cared about was public recognition over personal relationships. She believed that selfish men could never move beyond the glamour and their approval ratings into private moments with their loved ones. She was left alone, ignored, cast away, and believed that she would never be filled with love again. The emptiness within her was so deep — as deep as the well she visited each day at noon.

Though she enjoyed a short reprieve once a day at the well, she knew that to survive she had to keep going back there again and again to receive solace. She hoped against hope that maybe one day she would be loved. But all the signs indicated that she was not going to be accepted for who she was, that no one cared or would give her personal attention. Even her husband in the past never sacrificed his professional ambition to make a personal connection with her.

The Man at the Well

But one day at noontime, lost in her thoughts and walking toward the well, it happened. She was alone in her special space with the water jar by her side and heaviness in her heart, as she walked along. Then she saw a strange sight; someone was sitting by the well, the well that belonged to her people, and the one her ancestor Jacob had given to his son, Joseph. Fear gripped her heart. The man saw her. Puzzled and shocked, she moved forward cautiously toward the man. It was a step she would never regret because he had taken the first step toward her by being at the well — a step from his eternity to her eternity, a moment of emptiness and filling when two worlds collided.

At first glance, the man had the appearance of a religious scribe, perhaps a leader. He was not someone she wanted to meet during her private time. And she especially didn't want to have her time interrupted by a public figure that might have the same zealot passion as her husband. She didn't want her personal time of relaxation to be disturbed by haunting, hateful thoughts.

No, seeing the stranger was not a good sign. Her afternoon at the well wasn't going to go as planned. But with each step she took towards the well, her heart beat faster, and she sensed a different spirit surrounding this man. It was unusual, calm, and settling. Somehow, it was clear that he was there for *her*. The first exchange between them began with a humble request, not a demand as she was used to hearing. He requested a drink from her. He appeared to be a gentle, meek man who wanted to focus on her, not himself. It seemed he was powerful, yet he was using his power to seek her out and empower her — a weak and lost person seeking peace at the well. As she stood there before him, she felt safe, and for a moment unguarded, letting go of her fears and inhibitions.

On that scorching afternoon, meeting and talking with that stranger for the very first time, everything that she believed in broke apart and a bright light shone for the first time in and through her hard and shadowed self. The light pierced her wounded heart, soothing it like a balm from Gilead. For the first time, she felt that someone cared for her, and for the first time she felt that she never had to go back to the well again to be filled with peace or to quench her thirst. She wasn't feeling empty anymore, there was something strange springing forth within her, and she couldn't contain it anymore.

As she felt this new intense sensation inside, she could let go of the water jar that had become her comfort to ease her inner pain. For the first time in her adult life, she felt OK in her own skin, accepted in the presence of the rabbi. She felt joy, courage, and freedom flood into her being to let her be who she was created to be, and to be loved just the way she was. Someone was there to hear her who was fully aware of her dreams, her fears, and her mistakes. The warmth and kindness that she was experiencing was of such a pure spirit that it brought back the sweet memories of the wonderful and reassuring relationship that she had cherished with her now-deceased mother.

A refreshing spring of life within her was bursting forth like a fountain, and she couldn't keep it to herself. She went full throttle, running to town to tell the people what she had just experienced. She was so consumed with sharing the news that she not only forgot her water jar, she also forgot that she was running toward the very same people she had tried to stay away from, the ones that wanted nothing to do with her.

But now she couldn't get to the village fast enough to tell them about someone who came to her, waited on her, talked to her, and was interested in her. Someone who brought life and joy to her and would do the same for them. He changed her life from the inside out. It was what she had been seeking for years: to be heard by someone, to be personally cared for, and to be treated tenderly, not as an object but as a person with feelings, emotions, and needs.

As the empty well inside her began to fill up with hope and love, her spirit led her to go and tell the other people in the village. They were going through the same kind of pain and suffering that she was and they too needed to hear what the man had to say. People like her were also experiencing pain and rejection and taking refuge in their own type of "water jars" at the well. People like her had found only brief respites of peace. Isolated moments to express their true feelings and flee from the numbness of reality. Now, because of the man at the well, the unnamed woman had discovered a lifetime of harmony and acceptance, not just a temporary filling, and she was compelled to share the truth.

She ran to the village square and started shouting at the top of her voice like she had never done before and would probably never do again. She gave it all that she had, and everything from within her cried out as if her very soul was preaching. Initially, just a few people showed up to listen, but slowly and steadily the numbers increased until there was a large group who wanted to hear what she was saying. Those who had ignored her in the past paid attention. Those who had ridiculed and belittled her in the past kept quiet. Now she was speaking of something much bigger than herself. She was speaking of someone who had changed her, someone who could fill their lives the way he filled hers, and she wanted all of them to meet him. It was an open invitation; there was no caste preference or favored creed — everyone was welcome. The crowd started growing to hundreds, everyone leaving behind whatever they were doing. She was now in the middle of the crowd, yet she wasn't the center of attention. Rather, she was drawing everyone to the man she met, the one who was greater than Jacob and who was sitting at the well.

The Other Man

Meanwhile, right there in the public square, another meeting was taking place. It was her first husband Aleph's political rally. Being a sharp man, he seized the opportunity that the afternoon market square offered. He had already drawn a large crowd that day, as many saw him as a successful candidate who could fulfill the people's every request. He promised everyone a place to be heard and would even elevate women's status in society. (The irony was that his own wife had lost her status because of his life choices.) But still, people believed him and listened. They say people often have a short memory or just want to dismiss the past, so for many in the crowd, his personal life was separate from his public one. His speech was pleasant, well-crafted and written by the new woman in his life, who was supporting him and making sure that he would win the battle this time. She wanted to see him appointed as the next mayor of the town of Sychar, a position she saw as worth fighting for. A lot of promises were made today, many of which he probably wouldn't remember later or couldn't care less to keep.

While he was in the middle of delivering his speech, he sensed something unusual, and it was not just the heat. As he scanned the crowd, he noticed a few people leaving and moving to the other side of the street toward a dusty street corner. Initially, he thought there might be some emergency, but the stern look from his new wife encouraged him to continue with more intensity. He raised his voice and showered more promises. But soon, all his efforts were falling on empty chairs. He thought perhaps the townsfolk were not interested in his "uplift the women" program for the village, and maybe he should change the topic. But then he saw a large group of people had gathered on the other side.

Looking intently, he saw a figure that looked like a woman standing in the middle of the quickly forming crowd. She was shouting something about a man at the well. First, he was angry that someone would steal his crowd, but soon he saw that people were interested in what she was saying. She looked familiar, yet not. How could that be? As he was contemplating, he found that he was left standing alone and speaking to himself — even his wife had left him to hear what the other woman had to say! There was no choice for him but to wind up his half-delivered speech and make his way toward this stranger in town.

He was surprised by how many people were leaving him for this ordinary woman. But as he neared her, he got the shock of his life. He not only recognized her, he knew her very well. She was his first wife, the wife he had abandoned, and he was her first husband! A few years earlier he had chosen to reside in a different part of the village. He had moved on from the relationship and put her aside while focusing on his career and trying to win the prize he was vying for on the political stage. She was a forgotten past as far as he was concerned. And now here she was. He was surprised that she was even in the village at this time of day. She was in an unusual place, at an unusual hour of the day, and she was also, unusually, without her water jar, which was always in her possession. He could not believe what he was seeing!

As he saw her leading the crowd toward the well, he, surprisingly, followed along. In the back of his mind, he thought that perhaps she was causing this scene to get even with him or take revenge and defeat him from attaining his dream of political notoriety. As he walked with the crowd along the dusty road, he began to hear more of her message. It was about a stranger, a person she met at the well. He was curious to meet this man she was referring to. For a moment, he wondered, *Might this newcomer be his former wife's secret paramour?* Yet, her words didn't speak of things of this world, rather only about someone who came to change lives and give life.

Aleph, the first husband, had always been deeply convicted about what his life had become, always wanting to satisfy his ego with more votes and acceptance from the crowds. Now, strangely, his journey to the well caused within him a thirst that he couldn't ignore anymore. He wanted to hear more about this man. Aleph, the first husband, started listening carefully to the stranger, about what he was sharing. And over the next two days, he continued to listen, carefully, studying him for himself. He learned that this rabbi was humble, willing to give up public recognition and all the glory he deserved for the sake of a personal relationship with each person in the crowd. As time moved forward, Aleph's heart beat slower, relaxing into an unusual calm. He sensed a spiritual awakening within himself as he could see how foolishly he was filling his deep thirst with temporary and fleeting things of this world, focused primarily on recognition and popularity.

As he watched the rabbi, something strange and new was born within him. The first husband no longer needed to please everyone to feel accepted. Here was a man right before Aleph who crossed the cultural boundary to meet him personally. This stranger had left everything in heaven to tell and show humans how wonderfully and fearfully God Almighty created them. He came to explain that people do not have to re-create themselves or allow others to create them; they are incapable of doing so. The first husband learned that he didn't have to be someone else by trying to gain public acceptance, but that he could gain that only by accepting and living in favor of the Creator, who had made him beautiful to walk in abundant life.

Aleph listened to the man at the well. His spirit began to revive, his thinking began to renew, and his life began to change. A new man was being birthed. He didn't want to miss this opportunity, so he jotted notes on the back of his speech about everything that he had heard and learned from the rabbi. The following is what he wrote:

Judean Success

Aleph, the first husband, heard the man who was at the well talk about how the Hebrew people had a unique history of highs and lows, freedom and enslavement, owning it all and losing it all. And these first-century Jews were not an exception. They had experienced a major political crisis in their own land, losing power to a foreign government; they found themselves slaves in their own neighborhoods. The only thing they didn't want to lose was their religious heritage, supremacy, and power. And that was exactly what they felt was happening if the rumors were correct. The Pharisees, the religious frontrunners of the time, were taking notice of a new preacher in town who was gaining much popularity and name recognition. More people were coming to listen to him than attending their traditional temple services. More people were talking about this rabbi named Jesus than any other of their favorite rabbinic celebrities. This was indeed, as many would say, a Judean smash success, named by many as the "Elijah" who was supposed to come. This new wave was disquieting the customary religious culture and the status quo. Thus, he was not very well received by a few of the self-proclaimed custodians of the faith. The renewed passion and revival seen among the faithful were observed with suspicion. The new hope and vision found in Jesus's sermons were not going in the direction that the temple leaders were interested in.

While this newfound fear gripped the hearts and minds of the leaders and created panic among the temple guardians, Jesus was calling ordinary people to have a deeper relationship and a more intimate experience with their heavenly Father. Jesus was introducing a new concept of a relational God who was seeking an intimacy that traditions and ceremonies failed to provide; replacing the norms of the day was a challenge that was counter-cultural. Jesus, the man at the well, was bringing healing to the broken, giving hope to the oppressed, and leading a radical new ministry in this ancient land of Palestine. A true spiritual drought in the land was being quenched with water from an eternal life-giving spring. The thirst for God was being satisfied.

As crowds started to follow him everywhere and ministry opportunities were abundant, some people began to sense a ripe opportunity for themselves: a time to cash in on his rising profile and build a new empire. As this young rabbi attained high approval and seemed to be at the peak of his success, many experienced consultants were advising him to expand his reach and take it on to the global platform. New, catchy slogans were shouted from the rooftops, for example: "No soul wasted in hell anymore!" It was the messianic conquest, a time when the whole world could hear the good news. It was the right moment with the right momentum.

There was only one thing missing from totally capturing the frenzied crowd and turning his ministry into a mega-success. A simple nod from the preacher himself. Just a yes from him would have sent the message to the Palestinian scribe publishing houses to print hundreds of copies of his first book with his smiling picture on the front cover. That book would soon flood every newsstand in the Judean market square. But that nod never came. In fact, after a few days of preaching, the people could not find him anywhere! Did he disappear? Many people thought that he just vanished or may have slipped away among the Greeks. There was no trace of him.

*****

Amid much uproar among the crowds, we see a very different reaction from the rabbi Jesus. He had left the Judean countryside where he spent time with his disciples and baptized, and went to a town called Sychar in Samaria, an unknown place where he was an unwelcome, nameless nobody. His move was a total reversal of the common marketing strategies of that time and a slap in the face to all the widely-promoted business models. It seemed like a self-sabotaging approach, following an entirely different vision and purpose. The rabbi made a very clear statement by taking a surprising detour from the most sought-after road to success to a lesser-known highway, just to meet one unknown woman, who, if she had been given the choice, would have remained hidden.

Every one of the authors of several "steps to a successful ministry" books on the market would have gently told him how foolish and dangerous his move was. It wasn't the right time to ignore public demand and meet with an unknown and unnamed outcast of a rival community. And it is *never* wise to meet the enemy on their turf. If all he wanted to do was to set an example by taking care of the poor woman, it should have been done in front of the cameras, when the crowd was present or when they were eating the fried fish and warm garlic bread (surely it must have been the good stuff, right?) that had been miraculously multiplied from five loaves and two fish. As per many, going to Sychar reflected very poor judgment. They said: "You can't ignore the press" and "Networking with the right people will burnish your image and build a bright future." Was there a new image being introduced to people? Was he rebuilding a relationship factor that their self-absorbed lifestyle and a "me, myself and I" culture had demolished on the altar of self-aggrandizement?

Jesus ignored popular cultural practices and promotion strategies. His message was an upside-down one: the unpopular concepts of self-denial and emptying oneself by choosing personal relationships over public recognition or approval ratings. He considered relationship with one individual to be far more valuable than the adulation an entire community could offer him. The result that he preferred was to be present with and provide comfort to the person who was experiencing humiliation and suffering communal hatred. He chose the value of building a relationship with the person who was devoid of relationships rather than building on his own success. He gave higher priority to exalting a broken human life story over the breaking story of his own self-exalting campaign. He understood that this revolutionary concept of focusing on a personal relationship would empower each individual, restore every community, and heal all of humanity.

This rabbi, being sharply aware of the value of relationships, as well as the power of the healing touch and personal attention, chose to give up the expected marketing priorities of busyness and popularity for a less-desirable face-to-face meeting with a social outcast. Not to be seduced by the selfish desire to create his own identity, he identified with those whose identities were collapsing under the weight of neglect, abuse, and shame. Getting to know the story of one hurting soul gave him the strength to surrender the option of publishing a glamourized version of his story. His sacrifice brought transformation and peace to the one person who had almost given up on life and people.

It is easy to be in crowd-pleasing, fan-applauding mode and miss the soul-pleasing, spirit-serving moment of the one person. Sometimes we want to be in control and moving toward building a relationship can be risky and scary because it seems like we might lose control or not be in charge. We choose to be controlled by our insecurities and fears rather than to let go and be in the presence of another human who is hurting, fearful, and rejected. Exposing ourselves to others can bring our own fears to the surface; it is easier to hide in the corridors of fame and be accepted by the crowd than to be present with someone in their vulnerable and weak moments. Are we so afraid to encounter our true selves that we must run toward the crowd to hide?

Aleph, the first husband, paused for a moment; he could not take it anymore. As he wiped his tears, the guilt of his selfish lifestyle that had always sought popularity ripped his soul apart. At the same time, he was experiencing a fresh breath of stillness, a moment of warmth, forgiveness, and hope. He flipped the paper over to write some more words that he felt penetrating his very soul. He continued writing and filling the blank pages with his thoughts as well as the words coming forth from the lips of the rabbi.

Galilean Return

Aleph, the first husband, was running paper to write on, so he ran back to the market square to get more and then hurried back to the well. He didn't want to miss a single word of what the man was saying. What he heard next was powerful, and he wanted others in his community to learn, so he took careful notes. The first two words that were written on the new blank sheet were: "Galilean Return." Those words struck a chord within him because they meant that something very new was coming to his understanding, yet he was still so close to his old lifestyle. He had never been taught how to take the steps of sacrificing fame to have private and intimate relationships with other people in his life.

As he listened carefully, it made perfect sense to him. It was just like when Jesus was going back to Galilee. At the time of his return, the storm of dissension and spirit of competition were brewing, but it symbolized something much larger. Scripture says that Jesus learned that Pharisees were feeding on negative reports about him. An artificial competition was being created to bring animosity between these two ministries. They pitted the new rabbi Jesus against John the Baptist, one who was esteemed high by many though seemed less threatening. This climate was cultivated to deflect the shortcomings of the religious establishment and, in the process, kill the powerful ministries and the growing popularity of these two men. To everyone's surprise, Jesus made a bold move: to move away from being part of the controversy so as not to affect his ministry and his relationship with John. Along with success stories, Jesus did take time to heed to the opinions of those who were against this movement. He also knew the next best step. It indeed was a Galilean return.

People often want to surround themselves with success stories and therefore fail to hear and learn from those people who are not part of their camp. Jesus heard it all. When He found out what the Pharisees were saying, (even though the report was inaccurate), he was careful to make some necessary changes to his work that would not affect his purpose. He moved back to Galilee, where he began his work. It is not easy to take a break when you are at your peak, but if red flags are ignored, mishaps are certain to occur.

The first husband's notes seemed to slow down as his mind started to speed up. He remembered all those times when he didn't listen to what others said. He also remembered how he surrounded himself with yes-people and thus failed to see reality. He looked up again, and his eyes met the rabbi's. He was inviting Aleph to make that courageous journey back to his "Galilee."

Back to the Beginning

In the rabbi's overwhelming presence, Aleph, the first husband, started connecting those dots that led him to destroy the one vow that he had promised to keep, "till death do us part." His vision became clear as he captured what was happening in the rabbi's life. Aleph wrote: Jesus suddenly brought his thriving work in Judea to a complete stop and made his return to Galilee his important assignment, the place where he began. He went back to the place where he first announced his mission statement and purpose for coming to the world: "The kingdom of God is near...the acceptable year of the Lord's favor is here." He was less known then, but his message was heard clearly. He was unaffected by people's praise or misconceptions in those earlier days, so he wanted to go back. Rather than going with the flow, he cleared his mind of rumors, success, and competition. He retreated to find within him that soundless voice that was louder and clearer than any others on his journey.

It was important for him to return to where the mission was born — not just for him but also for those who first heard it and knew what he stood for. The people who were with him then and who understood him would stand with him when others could not discern truth when negative reports ran rampant. That is why it was important to go back to the beginning. Aleph's eyes filled with tears remembering how, instead of going back to his own woman, he went further away.

He took extra notes about how having such a place for every leader is important; without such a place you miss the bigger purpose of God. God wants his people to be intentional in revisiting the beginning, the Galilee of our life, to be rejuvenated, refreshed, and cradled for even a moment by the community that understands us. Sometimes society fails to provide such support to leaders. Sometimes people believe that work only happens when there is action, but action without a calm spirit is counterproductive, even destructive. Jesus modeled a powerful concept. Rather than attacking and correcting what the Pharisees were saying, he made a mid-course directional change. He willingly made changes to his itinerary to accommodate a new program so that he would not destroy what he was building.

The notes on the sheet of paper were yelling it aloud so that no one would miss this.

Detaching from People and Attaching to a Person

It was now more than just a few notes scribbled on a sheet. A profound impression was being made in the mind of this once ambitious politician. He wrote: "Removing yourself from the crowd to focus on a single person doesn't come easy. In fact, it becomes extremely difficult to give your total attention to someone when you are in a hurry to get things done and when your purpose gets stupefied. Among the busyness of life and bigness of activities, it seems impossible to drop things to meet with someone who may be breaking. Always being in a rush or in a hurry to satisfy our own selfish desires makes it hard to see someone who may have given up on life. To meet those who are at the point of breakdown, we need to break up with some of our self-serving demands and connections. Some of those habits and practices have become addictions and, in the riddance, we might experience withdrawals."

We need strong support and help to detach from lustful desires and the pride of life. Detachment is not easy unless we attach ourselves to the souls of other human beings, befriending and accompanying them to bring meaning and significance back into their lives. Creating a space for someone brings a purpose for ourselves as well as for others. One who is detached from oneself in a healthy way can invite others to detach from their own needs in order to offer and give help to those in need. Jesus here becomes our model in this selfless act of benevolence toward an ignored, neglected woman and an ignored, neglected community. A new chapter was beginning in Samaria.

When you have taken steps to lose your selfish self and have been redeemed, you can then model that new lifestyle for someone on a similar journey. You can call out to someone who is hurting and speak the truth to bring healing to the person's wounded self and soul — and then extend it to the community that collectively may be experiencing rejection, hurt, and pain. Few can show that kind of mercy boldly to someone who feels unworthy to receive it. Few are those who will accept the unacceptable members of society and have faith to believe that they can change. But those who have faith can walk that path to reconciliation and restoration for each of God's children.

Tired, Thirsty, Hungry

This alternative route Jesus chose to return to Galilee came with a price. Walking through the unfamiliar territory clearly tired him, and the scorching noon sun above was merciless, increasing his thirst. Food had not yet arrived, as the disciples had gone to the nearby town. Weary from his travel and thirst, he came to a well, and he sat down there expecting someone to come and give him water. God the Incarnate could identify completely with the human experiences of tiredness, thirst, and physical exhaustion — the need to sit down and regain his strength. He came to a place where he knew his body could not take him any further without some cool water to drink and some time to rest.

Are these feelings and physical limitations familiar? Do we feel guilty about being tired? Do we feel guilty about taking a break? Do we just keep going and going until we collapse? Why are we so caught up in doing rather than being? Why can't our culture appreciate rest? Do we thirst and feel that no one understands us?

The God of the universe on the dusty road to Samaria experienced every human emotion that we experience when we get tired on our life journey. This was a moment when Jesus was vulnerable and exhibited the exhaustion and weakness any human body and mind can suffer. He did not put on a fake front, blustery strength and machismo and deny the reality of his experience. He sat down and took a break, a pause from his journey to rest. His sitting was symbolic of him identifying with the tiredness of our souls. He did it to remind us to stop moving when life becomes hard. He showed us a better way to sit, pause, seek, be refreshed, and be found.

*****

Time with Jesus

It was the end of the second day, and the teacher was ready to leave the well and move on to his destination. Although Samaria was not part of his official itinerary, he made this deliberate diversion to spend time with people who his own community despised. He took the time to be with an unnamed woman and with her people who had a very different way of practicing their faith. He left behind a new set of ideas and a different way of living life. He taught them an important lesson: to be inclusive and respectful of others and to be unafraid of meeting and loving people who are different. As this Sychar community came together and listened to the teacher, they connected with each other — to their history and to the new culture of hope and eternal life that he was preaching about. The time with Jesus helped the community to experience healing in a new way, forgiveness as never before, and an opportunity to correct a lack of understanding that had prevented them from living life to the fullest.

Aleph, the first husband, paused his writing and looked up to see the teacher saying farewell to those who had gathered to listen to his words. For the first time, reality sunk in. The first husband never thought his life could change so dramatically and so drastically in such a short time. All his life, he had passionately pursued a path that he felt would make him complete and fulfilled, but instead, it led to emptiness, selfishness, and hurt. Even now, trying to gather the pieces of broken relationships and his first marriage and making every effort to make it look good from the outside weren't helping him. Inside he was still thirsty, going back again and again to the same empty source to satisfy his thirst: seeking people's approval, vying for a position of power and authority, and somehow making his life seem to have a purpose.

But today, standing there, life made much more sense; it appeared the right priorities were falling into place. For the very first time, he was giving up the fight within himself — to be recognized and be popular did not feel cool anymore. He was experiencing a new desire to focus on people and to value personal relationships. People became his priority and helping them find life's true meaning became his objective. He felt like for the first time he was going in the right direction. He didn't have to abuse and sideline others to advance himself.

The two days with the teacher were a special treat, a spiritual retreat. It had become a time of restoration, a breakthrough. For a moment, standing there among the thinning crowd, Aleph felt sad to see the teacher leave. At the same time, he felt empowered, confident, and grateful that he could spend two full days in fellowship with the rabbi Jesus. These were days he would not soon forget. In his hands, he was holding papers filled with the most powerful words he had ever heard — words that turned his life upside down.

He knew that there were many in his village and among his people who needed to hear the truths that Jesus spoke. He decided to commit his life to practice and then preach what he had learned. He also knew in his heart that things had changed for him because he chose to take two days away from his busyness to spend time with the teacher. He had been intentional. That effort led him to live his life as a reflection of what he experienced. He chose to go to the well to receive the living water flowing from the rabbi Jesus.

He felt a special bond with those who had stood alongside him as he listened to the teacher, others who were also changed by his words. But first he went home and shared what he experienced with his own family and his children. Then he decided to go and meet those who had a similar experience. He felt an urge to connect and hear what they had to share about their encounter with Jesus. He felt peace for the first time just being himself. He felt good about others in his life. He felt gratitude welling up within him for all his relationships.

As he was preparing to meet the others, he heard a knock at the gate of his home. He walked over to see who it was. As he opened the gate, he was surprised but happy to see the man who was standing there. Together they sat down in the guest room and, sipping the tea freshly prepared by his wife, he listened carefully to what the guest had to say. The guest was holding papers that looked like business documents, but on the back of the papers were some scribbled notes. The guest looked down at the papers and paused for a moment. He seemed lost in a memory. The pause ended quickly, and then he spoke for the next 30 minutes.

In the next chapter, we will meet this stranger who came to visit Aleph, the first husband, and hear about his life, his story, and learn what was scribbled on the back of the papers in his hand.

Chapter 3

Denying to Giving

The Samaritan woman said to Him, "You are a Jew, and I am a Samaritan woman. How can you ask me for a drink?" (For Jews do not associate with Samaritans) (John 4:9).

Beit's Story

If anybody could point a finger at what went wrong with Beit, the best guess would be his stepfather. Looking back, Beit would have to admit that he never seriously tried to get along with his stepfather. His own father had died in a farm accident when his mom was pregnant with Beit. It was a terrible time for his mother; she had to go through a pregnancy and give birth while dealing with her husband's death. Not having a father around who loved him scarred Beit. Some of his friends and relatives often wondered why he remained such a quiet and reserved kid. He resolutely shut people out of his life and for those he could not, he avoided.

Because Beit was so cautious about who he allowed into his life, he didn't have many friends growing up. The only person he didn't mind spending time with was his mother. He became her companion and helper. When most boys his age would be out getting dirty playing in the dusty courtyards, Beit would be walking with his mother from the bazaar carrying cloth satchels full of her purchases. For Beit, his mother was everything he had, and he enjoyed being close to her.

Some years later, his mother went to work for the man his father had once worked for. Things started changing at home when one of her bosses began courting her, and soon the couple started speaking seriously about uniting in marriage. From the outset, Caleb was unacceptable to Beit. First, because he took his mother's attention away from her beloved son, and second, he brought his three older children into their new home. Beit didn't like the idea of being the youngest in the house, but even more, he hated the idea of losing his mother's attention to a strange man.

Though he wanted his mother to be happy, deep down he believed that the cost of losing her was too high. He found every reason not to welcome his mother's new husband and refused to accept him as a father in his life.

Caleb belonged to a different community, and Beit felt it was not right for his mother to be united with someone who looked differently, believed differently, prayed differently, and came from a different town. Beit denied his stepfather access to his life and, rather than giving him a chance, he chose not to interact with him whenever possible. Beit ignored every sincere effort and rejected every attempt at friendship Caleb made. Beit's resentment toward Caleb marked the beginning of his troubles. He grew up to become an angry man and harbored a lot of pain and hurt within himself. He also began to develop animosity toward others who didn't belong in "his" group, venting his suppressed anger in the form of discrimination and prejudice against certain "others."

Over the years Beit grew up, worked hard, and eventually opened his own bakery. Even though the business could have been very prosperous due to its strategic location in the bazaar, it never saw much success. His business maintained itself, generating enough money for survival, but not enough for any kind of quality living. Many of his friends and neighbors privately opined that he would have been more prosperous had he been more open, inclusive, and if he would have catered to all people and all communities. But he refused to deal with people outside his own faith and community, preferring to lose them as customers rather than doing business with them.

His wife recognized his stubbornness, and she often tried to correct him, but he did not give her ideas and thoughts any serious consideration. Instead he rebuked her and looked down upon her, accusing her of being too greedy and willing to compromise his values to earn more money. For a long time, she tolerated him, but she didn't want their two boys to grow up having the same kind of intolerance. So, even at the risk of facing an angry husband, she allowed her boys to play and make friends with children from different social, cultural, racial, and religious backgrounds.

They say that things got worse on an afternoon when a few of her sons' friends from a different community came to their house and asked Beit's wife for something to drink. Without a moment's hesitation, she reached for the water jar and poured a drink for the tired, thirsty children. As she handed them the clay-cups, her husband walked into the room. He erupted. First, he was repulsed by seeing those children in his home. Second, he felt his authority had been disrespected and discredited, and his values disregarded in his own home. He ranted and raved and caused a terrible scene for everyone to see. He rebuked his wife in front of the frightened children. The incident was the beginning of the end of the relationship between Beit and his wife. It was a constant reminder of the significant difference in their way of thinking.

Beit would not give up what he believed. As days went by he become angrier and even less open to relenting his position. Instead of seeking help, he chose to suffer and hurt himself and those around him. What he had experienced in the past was affecting him and others. Thus, his wife made the difficult choice to leave him and, along with their sons, moved back home with her parents. Her actions were not received well within her community. People pointed fingers at her for the shame she caused her husband and brought upon her family. For this woman, having two failed marriages and being the talk of the town affected her in every way. Lonely once again, and being rejected and misunderstood by others, took a toll on her body and mind, causing her to suffer from serious depression and illness.

The Unnamed Woman

As we understand this unnamed woman a bit more deeply, we can understand the pain she experienced from failed marriages, which carried over into how she treated others:

When a Samaritan woman came to draw water, Jesus said to her, "Will you give me a drink?" (His disciples had gone into the town to buy food.) The Samaritan woman said to him, "You are a Jew and I am a Samaritan woman. How can you ask me for a drink?" (For Jews do not associate with Samaritans.) John 4:7-9

Rather than responding immediately by pouring water from her jug to give to the thirsty man at the well, her reaction was tempered by her past experiences, the pain, hurt, anger, and disappointments in her life. She was a victim of husbands who had treated her harshly. She didn't know there was a better way to respond to the man at the well. But then she met someone who, even after being opposed and oppressed, didn't react or hit back but remained as silent as a lamb taken to slaughter. This attitude was foreign in her world, especially from a man. But that is exactly what happened at the well.

*****

It was about noon, and usually people did not go to the well at that time of the day unless they intentionally wanted to avoid people. And that's exactly why the unnamed Samaritan woman decided to go at that hour: to avoid the people who had made her life miserable. And she had a good reason to do so.

Jesus, after a long walk in the burning sun, and being tired and thirsty, sat down by the well to rest. Seeing a woman coming with her water jar, he asked her for a drink. She had the rope to lower the water jar to fetch the water from the well and thus was capable of giving him a drink. Even though she was from a different community and he was a Jew, when he was thirsty he asked her for a drink. He didn't allow human prejudice to prevent him from asking for help. He didn't allow the pride of being a religious rabbi stop him from talking with a woman. He asked for help and was willing to appear as a needy and helpless traveler without embarrassment. The God of the universe humbled himself to a position of being disadvantaged.

Do we stop to ask for help from him, or do we remain silent when help is at hand?

Request Denied

Had this been a normal encounter, the woman would have seen a tired, thirsty man, and graciously offered to serve him a drink of water. Perhaps she might have said, "Sir, I would be pleased to lower my water jar into the well with this rope and draw up a drink for you." But no! She didn't offer him a drink.

Rather, she was shocked at the audacity of this man who dared to ask for a drink from a woman who was a Samaritan.

Jesus, being tired, thirsty, and sitting in the scorching, noontime sun, was making a very reasonable request. But the woman was surprised. The reason for her surprise was that he was a Jew, and she was a Samaritan. She explained to him: "We do not belong to the same group, we are different, so your need cannot be met. Differences in the way we believe and the places we worship prevent me from fulfilling your need. You do not belong; therefore, you are not welcome to share with us." She made it even clearer by adding: "The differences between us are so great that even disrespecting basic human needs such as thirst will be all right and don't make any difference to me." The woman justified her inhumane action of withholding kindness to a stranger (which is inappropriate in any culture, even more so in hers). She could assert her personal bitterness against men by using the cover of religious difference.

Does this ever happen to us, or is this just an incident from a distant time and place?

As humans what we have in common is that we bear the image and likeness of our Creator, yet we still focus on differences created by human fear, hurt, and greed.

Why is she reacting this way? What does she think will happen if she gives him the water? Why is she afraid to be kind or generous to a stranger? Is it easier to give into fear than to be merciful?

Her explanation may include how her community of Samaritans experienced years of oppression at the hands of the Jews. Maybe she felt entitled to repay evil by not giving Him water. For the first time, she was in control and in charge of the future of a Jew. Perhaps she thought, *My people and I have been victimized, so I will make him a victim of suffering, too.* Was she being nationalistic or was there something bigger than that at play? Let us take a closer look at the life of this woman to gain an understanding of her actions and behavior and her lifestyle pattern.

Past and Pain

The pain and trauma she experienced at the hands of other people may have numbed her to the pain and trauma of other people. Insensitivity and cruelty came easily. Unknowingly, she was feeding into the cycle of pain, perpetuating and paying it forward. Until Jesus stepped in. Even when he was denied the water and was made to suffer the pain she carried within her, and even though he was undeserving of such treatment, he did not hurt her in response. Rather, he was willing to offer her what he had, and he extended an invitation to her for a kinder, deeper, and more meaningful life.

Her past influenced her present behavior. This is often how people justify their inhumane treatment of others. *Our past experiences often limit our abilities to act on both new and present opportunities for us to serve others.* Our past also has the power to destroy future hope, as well as stop the natural flow of kindness, joy, and love that streams from soft human hearts. Only until a distinctly different future is made visible and possible by the power of the Almighty, can forgiveness, love, and hope spring forth and overtake our past negative experiences.

How often do people unknowingly play the "victim game" because they had an unhappy childhood and then go on to become part of the greater evil that exists within our society? How often do children pick up attitudes of hate and abuse from within their home and pay that behavior forward toward their peers and their own families later in life? When we don't let go, the past preys on us. Some people believe that they will feel better or that they can make things right if they just accept the status quo. Other people find a strange sort of pleasure in harboring a grudge because it allows them to have a handy excuse for inflicting pain. Whatever the cause, human nature dictates that if we are not personally able to pay back a hurt, we will make sure that it is paid forward somehow. The cycle will continue until someone steps onto a different path and chooses a different way of living, a different way of being human.

Control and Power

When the Samaritan woman denied Jesus a drink of water, she believed that she held the power because she controlled the resources. The well belonged to her community, but the rope and the water jar belonged to her. In her eyes, Jesus was dependent on her, and because of his dependency, she was going to control him. She was going to make him pay for the mistakes of his people, the Jews. This was her opportunity to become the representative of her people and to make Jesus compensate for his community's faults. She felt by making him suffer she would somehow ease the pain of the Samaritans' past.

But Jesus showed her a new and profound way of establishing true justice without offense and hurt, but rather by sacrifice and understanding. He was still willing to pour out everything he had even when he was denied a cup of water. He was prepared to give up everything for the woman, despite his people's strained and painful history. He did not respond the way she did — he was compassionate. She had never known that there could be a different way to react or redemption. Justice without violence or negativity was not what she had learned, and justice through forgiveness was both a revelation and revolution.

How often do we see similar thought patterns operating within our own people, family, or maybe within us? Our culture at large speaks of getting even, taking revenge, hurting others, or making them pay for what they did. When atrocities are propagated within a community, a cancer of suffering and pain spreads throughout. It continues until someone steps in and is willing to turn the other cheek when slapped (see Luke 6:28-30).

The unnamed woman suffered much at the hands of her husbands, her own people, and the Jews. Even if she ignored the pain she received from her community, she could not forget the suffering at the hands of her own loved ones; it caused pain she could not forget. The trauma she experienced because of husbands and the way her sons had to suffer was also part of her story. No one was willing to hear her story, no one was kind to her. So, when all this pain accumulated within her and had no healthy release, it came out of her as anger towards this innocent stranger.

Have any strangers ever left us with a similar experience or have some of our closest friends and family members experienced this hurtful behavior from us?

When she walked to the well that day, she was looking forward to some peace; instead she saw a Jew sitting there occupying her sacred place. Her anger flared, and she inflicted it on an unsuspecting, defenseless, tired, and thirsty man. Because no one listened to her and she had always been treated as a nobody, she subconsciously felt that her inhumane action toward the stranger would get her noticed, heard, and maybe even accepted.

Does this kind of unheard, unnoticed pain ever emanate from us?

But, ironically, it wasn't the townspeople who accepted her; it was this strange rabbi Jesus who was willing to accept her just as she was. He was even willing to take her offensive behavior. He did not react. He was kind and willing to hear her out and be gracious. He was willing to show her what she was missing by being unforgiving, angry, hurtful, and hateful. He was willing to work through her pain and lead her into a place of comfort that she lacked because of the way her husbands and others had treated her.

After talking with Jesus, for the first time she was shown how to handle pain and suffering. She was excited and ready to share this new experience with her people. No more was she going to keep hurting and hating; now she was going to pour out what was poured into her. She began to feel love, forgiveness, and hope well up within her and wanted to share it with her community. Now, for the first time in her life, the wheels of compassion were turning, and the wheels of the cycle of pain were slowly coming to a halt.

How often have we seen or known people with bright futures lose control and hurt people who had nothing to do with their pain and suffering? The pain they carried within made them think it was legitimate or all right to take it out on others; somehow, they thought their actions were justified or would bring relief. Too often these days we hear the news of someone walking into a school and killing innocent children because the person was angry or felt mistreated or unheard. Their festering anger brings grief to countless people. The entire community suffers when people who are suffering are not cared for or heard. Anger spreads like an infection until someone moves in and is willing to listen, to hear about a person's suffering, accept them, walk with them without judgment, and bring healing to one person, two people, and eventually to the whole community.

The Counter Offer

> *"Sir," the woman said, "you have nothing to draw with, and the well is deep. Where can you get this living water? Are you greater than our father Jacob, who gave us the well and drank from it himself, as did also his sons and his livestock?"* John 4:11-12

When the unnamed woman asked, *"Are you greater than our father Jacob?"* she was saying: unless you are someone important, you cannot get the water. She was telling Jesus he lacked resources, so he was not great enough or smart enough. She was telling him that he was weak, because he could not satisfy his thirst without the necessary things. She was trumpeting her superiority: "I control the well, and I will not give you water because you do not belong to us, and you are not greater than our father, Jacob."

Human needs don't matter or are minimized when people are selfish and allow past greatness and current resources to dictate actions. By our actions, we often control and hold power over others — for good or for bad.

Do we value greatness over compassion?

Jesus told the woman, *"If you knew ... who it is that asks you for a drink, you would have asked him, and he would have given you living water."* Jesus said that he gave eternal water without discrimination. He wanted her to know that his ego, his greatness, or his suffering were not barriers. He said he would give to all who ask, without bias or profiling. He is able to give because he knows that the water can wash away their past hurts.

In John 7:37-38, Jesus cried out, saying, *"Let anyone who is thirsty come to me and drink. Whoever believes in me, as Scripture has said, rivers of living water will flow from within them."* This water is not for those who belong to a certain sect but for *anyone* who comes to Jesus with a thirst. He guarantees that *anyone* who drinks the water he gives will never thirst again. Coming thirsty was the only criterion. This was an offer that the woman at the well, her community, and indeed the world had never heard before. It was (and still is) an open invitation to all who are weary, heavy laden, and need rest (see Matthew 11:28).

Everyone can qualify, and anyone is welcome to receive freely. Jesus's offer was counter-cultural, one that would bring healing not only to the woman and her people but to the whole world. Over 2,000 years ago, the joyful words "Come thirsty, ask, and be filled" were uttered at the well for the first time, and they echo around the world to this day. No one should stand afar anymore; *anyone* can come close to God and receive him. We are *always* invited; you don't have to thirst anymore — you can come and drink deeply of his living water.

Beit, the Second Husband

The unnamed woman's second husband, Beit, had some serious issues that caused severe problems not only in his professional life but also in his home life. Sometimes when we don't deal with negative personal matters, they can take hold not only deep within us but have serious consequences for others. As we are growing up, they can become stumbling blocks not only for ourselves but also for other people's growth and human flourishing. The second husband was going through a difficult time in his business career because he harbored resentment. He begrudged how the Jews unfairly called him impure and unholy. He refused to associate with them and even refused to do business with them. He thought that his dissociation would be an appropriate punishment for the unfairness and ill treatment.

When he refused orders from Jewish customers, it was almost pleasurable. He had the power to inflict pain on the Jewish community in response to what they had done to him and his people over the years. This decision affected his business, and it began to suffer, yet he would not change his behavior. Frequently, when negative behavior and attitudes are not corrected, our inner pain dictates our outward actions and becomes the catalyst for more pain. In his case, his untreated pain created anger that resulted in discriminatory behavior and caused financial stress over the years. His accountant had repeatedly warned him about his finances being in the red, yet he did not change. The people to whom he owed money would harass him for payment and it often embarrassed his family. His wife bore most of the stress. She wanted to help, but her hands were tied, and she was forced to endure this anxiety-filled situation.

Often, to escape the niggling debt collectors, his wife would hide. She would turn down social invitations to avoid being part of common assemblies of her community. This isolated her, and she felt suffocated and didn't know how to express it. So, the anger within her found an easy target — her own people. It became so severe that she hated everybody and blamed others for what she was going through. She had married the man thinking he would be more understanding, but it turned out that he was a bigot who he was unable to provide for the family's needs. Even her children were mocked in school for being so poor and for having to live off of other people's handouts.

Since she constantly lived in fear of getting caught by creditors, she always returned to her special hiding place. It was her way of escaping the world which was against her. At the well, she felt safe. Being in her own little world away from others was the only place and time that she could be free. She cleverly chose the time when others were busy or resting in the coolness of their homes. The hot sun didn't matter — she would have the well to herself. That's how she saw herself and her inner life: under great heat and restless. Being at the well gave her a brief break from all those who were after her money, her life, and her sanity. Her problems did not matter a bit to them and they didn't care who she was. They just wanted what was owed.

And so, it is today; we have become a people who value money over the value of human beings. Money blinds us to such an extent that we forget to see the pain, fail to listen to the sufferings, and ignore helping the poor and needy. In the process of living our self-centered lives, we cease to be the humans God intended us to be, especially when we trample his people, their dignity, and destroy their spirits with our own selfishness.

A Soft Voice

Today, as she was approaching the well and feeling grateful in her heart for a break from the harassers, she looked up and was crestfallen that someone was already at the well. Fear gripped her heart. Could this be a credit collector waiting for her? She was worried and upset that this stranger appeared to be Jewish. From a distance, he looked like a traveler who was tired and maybe thirsty from a long journey. At the same time, he carried himself as a man on a mission. She also assumed that this upper-caste Jew would not humble himself to ask her, a lowly Samaritan, for a drink. Her past experiences and her husband's prejudice taught her that the man would rather die from thirst than ask someone like her for help.

But as she got closer she was shocked to hear a soft voice, a very different kind of voice, asking her for a drink. In that very moment when she heard the request, she let the anger of the past overtake her, the anger for what she had suffered at the hands of the Jewish community, who she felt were responsible for everything bad that had ever happened to her. Even now, her husband's negative behavior because of his anger against the Jewish community affected her. His actions had led her to fend for herself and her children alone.

Now, she had the perfect time and place to unleash her anger. As the saying goes: "if you can't name your pain then you can't change your pain." There was no other place where she could release everything that had built up within her for so long. She would represent her community and avenge all the hurts that they had faced at the hands of the Jews. By denying the rabbi a drink and thus tormenting him she could bring some justice to her people. Although even though she felt the pain that her own community had inflicted upon her, she still chose them over this man at the well.

It is both ironic and sad to see how the pain that we suffer causes us to display the same attitudes and behaviors that we abhor in others. The unnamed woman despised how her husband had discriminated against people of other communities, and she saw how it affected others, but now in her own anger, she was doing the same.

But to her surprise, the rabbi did not react negatively to her response to his request. Rather, he accepted her without judgment, giving her the opportunity to vent the pain she was harboring within. He respectfully waited for her to finish talking and then acknowledged her true feelings. Never had she encountered such a response, especially from a man. Shocked, she waited for him to speak.

As he began to speak, she quickly realized that he wasn't the evil Jewish person she thought he was, but instead he was a loving man who could receive all her questions without taking offense. She felt all her pain and hurt fading away. She had met someone who was asking her to "cast her burden upon him" and assuring her that he would sustain her. Somehow, she knew that everything was going to be fine.

The encounter was surreal for her. She slowly began to loosen her grip on the water jar, which she had grasped firmly in her hands, the very same jar she had refused to use to draw water for him. She placed it next to the well. She stepped away from it and felt everything that was holding her in her world of shame and negativity losing its grip on her. She felt perfectly fine for the very first time — able to breathe deeply and confident to handle her world, her people, and her problems. Her fears were gone. She could not stop feeling the love that was overtaking her at that moment. She was experiencing his peace that surpassed all her understanding.

Standing near Jacob's well, she strangely felt less burdened and less stressed. There was such an overflowing warmth surrounding her that she even forgot why she was there in the first place. Her pain, anger and resentment were not important anymore. She knew there was someone who knew everything that she had gone through and everything that she was experiencing — and still loved her. The rabbi did not have a condemning spirit. Everything about him welcomed and beckoned her into a new way of living. This was a sacred moment for her, and she wanted to bask in it forever.

Good News to Share

But then she remembered her family and she thought about her children. She thought about all her friends who were experiencing similar anxiety, pain, and anger. She knew she had to run and tell everybody about this strange man, the prophet and the Savior of the whole world whom she just met. Was he just that or was he more than that? It was a question that she wanted to put out there in front of her people. So she left her water jar — the symbol of everything she was holding onto inside, the anger, pain, the past, history, failure, rejection, and loss — at the foot of the well. She ran as fast as she could toward the market square; it was a little after the noon hour. She knew by this time people would have finished shopping and would be getting ready to go back home.

She also knew that many of the shoppers would be going home with heavy hearts. For many in the community, even living an ordinary life was difficult. So she had to run quickly, as she had good news to share. On her way she noticed a group of Jewish religious people, perhaps disciples of a teacher, coming toward her carrying food. They looked at her surprised as she ran past, but that didn't bother her — not today. She didn't stop to speak to them. She was on a mission. She was not hungry nor was she thirsty because she had just tasted the bread of life and had drank living water. This living water was something the people of the village didn't know about, but she knew it was the time of quenching. She had to tell them about the new life she had discovered.

Meanwhile, in the village near the market square, life proceeded as normal, except she could hear a political rally being held nearby. At the second husband's bakery, no one had come in to buy anything all day. If another day ended without a sale, Beit knew very well he would have to sell the business. The street was quiet. Even the usual synagogue-going kids didn't pass by. Beit was getting worried, wondering where the people were. Lost in these thoughts, he saw a man coming toward his shop quickly. He was happy at the thought of a customer approaching his deserted bakery.

All kinds of thoughts were going through Beit's mind: maybe this customer would place a big order that would give him that much-needed financial break, maybe the man was going to order for a wedding party, or maybe...? Soon the man appeared right at the front door with an odd look and hastily said: "Your ex-wife is here, and she's talking about him. She is taking everyone there." That is all Beit could decipher before the man raced away. His ex-wife? She's talking about who? And she is taking everyone where? Everyone who?

Beit was trying to make sense of what the man said. His ex-wife who had moved out on him? What new trick could that no-good woman be up to now? What in the world was she doing here? While he was still standing in shock, the man ran down the street toward a large crowd and left Beit trying to piece the puzzle together. The man joined the crowd that was following a woman, the one who was once his woman. Beit realized that there wasn't going to be any business that day, so he hung the "closed" sign, locked the door behind him and hurried to join the crowd.

Pushing people aside, he slowly worked his way through the crowd and got closer to his ex-wife. He was shocked once again to see her leading the very people who had frightened her and treated her poorly! One thing he knew very well about his ex-wife: at this time of the day she shouldn't be here in the market. She should be alone holding her water jar at her favorite spot: Jacob's well. He was even more surprised to see that she didn't have her water jar. He knew that meant she hadn't been at the well that day. If she hadn't gone to the well, then where had she gone and what was all this commotion about?

Standing there confused, Beit looked up and saw his ex-wife going toward the path that led to the well. He knew this place very well because that was where they had their final and most difficult argument. It was the place where she told him how she had been hurt because of his behavior and how she wanted him to change for the sake of their kids and family. She had pleaded with him to be more accepting of people from other communities, to ignore the differences and work together. She had asked him to change so that his business would become profitable and get out of debt. If only he had heeded her wise direction, things would have been different and better.

Silently, this baker followed his ex-wife to the well. During his journey along the road toward the well, a million thoughts and questions were going through his mind: Why did she look so strangely happy? What was at the well? Why are all these people following her when they didn't even like her? What could be so important? Then, from a distance, he saw a stranger sitting at the well. The man didn't appear to belong to his community. He watched his ex-wife run toward the stranger with so much joy! It was a joy that he had never witnessed before. Then his eyes caught a peculiar sight: her water jar left alone at the well.

He stepped closer to the well and examined the abandoned water jar. His mind still wandering, he asked himself an important question: *What made her give up her water jar, which represented hatred, discouragement, and disagreement with her people?* He knew her enough to know that the water jar had symbolized the anger, regret, guilt, and pain of her past. The anger had become part of her, as did the prejudice he had instilled into their home. She had become someone she had never wanted to be and that made her ashamed and brimming with self-hatred.

As Beit stood there, something pulled him towards the teacher. It was magical, peaceful, and spiritual. He couldn't contain himself nor could he ignore the overwhelming presence of something supernatural around him and within him. Then the baker heard the powerful yet respectful words of the rabbi, words that pierced his heart. As he listened, he heard words of acceptance and love that he had never heard before. He broke down within himself as he stood near the well and the water jar. Although one of many among the crowd, he seemed to be left all alone with his thoughts about what this teacher was saying. He knew this was a life-changing moment, so he took out his business papers and started taking notes on the back of them. He scribbled down everything he heard that day and the following day as he sat along with others listening to this wholly unique master-teacher. Then he walked back to his home.

In the evening, when he was all alone, he pulled the papers out of his pocket and read them. His thoughts went back to the days when he was lonely and how he resented everything and everybody. He knew he had spread his hatred and prejudice to others and stood condemned as he realized his sins. But today there was a healing happening within him. He could not stop his tears from flowing; he felt such a deep sense of relief. He was completely consumed with love for all, especially those who were different from him. He even wanted to ask for forgiveness from his stepfather for all the years of ignoring his attempts to grow close. It was still dark outside his home in Sychar, yet there was a bright light bursting within him. The sun had nearly risen when he finally lifted his eyes from his writings. From his experience with the teacher, he had written down the following points on the back of his unused business paper.

A Necessary Journey

Beit was thoroughly surprised that the rabbi had journeyed to an unwelcoming destination like Sychar. He had crossed the boundary that the two communities (Jews and Samaritans) had created over many generations. He broke the wall that was erected because of the hatred between them. The Scriptures say that "Jesus had to go" (through Samaria) and it was something that he could not ignore (John 4:4). It was an important assignment that he would not let slip by or postpone. This encounter seemed to be an urgent issue of the highest priority. How could meeting a woman who was a nobody ever be a major task for such a high-profile person?

It was a purposeful journey because most Jews avoided going through Samaria. They thought Samaritans were impure people who had rejected the faith. The stigma dated back to the time when Israel had been divided into two kingdoms, the north and the south, and that had happened later when foreign kings attacked them. Most of the northern kingdom inhabitants were exiled; those who remained were married to Gentiles. Thus they became a hybrid people called "Samaritans." Jews considered themselves to be holier and purer than Samaritans. Therefore, they avoided any contact with them. But it was exactly to this Samaritan community that Jesus intentionally went. He was determined to undo the tension between the two communities by reaching out to both. His intention was to teach them a lesson that both sides were missing because of their anger.

Why did Jesus consider this route necessary? Jesus was making a new way. He was following a different kind of passion, a purpose with a very determined mindset that was counter-cultural. He walked into a place of hatred, but he very strategically moved toward creating peace with an unnamed woman who was conflicted within herself and with her people.

Even though it was an unwelcoming neighborhood for Jews, he came offering the gift of living water to any hurting soul who would ask. This was a new way of living in the spirit of humility. It was uncomfortable territory for a Jew and much harder for a rabbi. He offered someone — who was per the norms of the day considered a prostitute — the opportunity to become a different person. He made her into a woman who was comfortable and at peace with herself, her people, and her faith.

Beit could no longer bear the situations in his life. He'd suffered many sleepless nights because of his failed marriage and unsuccessful business, but what he heard from Jesus made him sleepless in a different way: he was excited about a new way of living. He would live his life for the sake of others, being a peacemaker rather than being a peace "breaker." He would be the one who would be able to bring people together rather than keeping them apart. He wanted to give up hatred and live a life of compassion. He knew he had missed out on living a good life and having a stable family because of his deep-seated prejudice and misguided priorities. He decided to give up everything that was unproductive and chose to be more like the new visitor in town, the One his ex-wife had introduced to the community. He read more from his notes — drinking in the living water that flowed from the pages into his soul. He wanted to make sure that he understood everything that Jesus said as he spoke to the crowd (speaking to each individual as if they were an audience of one).

Walk into the Mess, Step into the Unclean

The more Beit heard Jesus speak, the more he was surprised at the way the rabbi lived his life. He knew in his heart that this man was obviously greater than any prophet before him. The way he explained events of the past and the future made him no less than the Messiah they were waiting for. Jesus walked into the unwelcoming city of Samaria, considered a forsaken place by many. For a rabbi to step onto the ground of an unclean people would make him ceremonially unclean. Why would he do this? What was his purpose? The only good answer that Beit could come up with was: because he wanted to show who God is and reveal his purpose to humanity. Jesus was willing to step into the mess and uncleanness to create a safe place. He didn't walk away because of others' opinions or traditions. He walked the path that led to the restoration of humankind, redeeming people from their own selfishness and stopping them from being alienated from God and his purpose.

By this time the sun was shining brightly in the sky, and Beit continued to learn more about the man at the well from the living water that was now refreshing him with truth. He went on to read more of what he had written.

Identifying with Those Who Have No Identity

Jesus chose to isolate himself from the crowd to be with one who was isolated herself. He couldn't, and he wouldn't, ignore the one who was forgotten, and that's why he took that lonely road until he found her. The distance that had been created by human ideologies and differences marginalized some. Those who didn't follow the status quo were pushed out of the circle. These people were not invited to the common gatherings and were outcasts. But the rabbi Jesus moved with compassion to seek those who were lost and denigrated. Jesus came seeking them; he took that road and met her. He waited for her and, by doing so, Jesus demonstrated how God waits for us, seeks us out, and how often he is found at the most unlikely places.

Beit paused for a moment to let this reality permeate his heart. He wanted this truth to sink in so that he would never again treat others with contempt or disrespect. He felt an extraordinary sense of being washed within his inner being and his soul.

Coming Near

As Beit's understanding about God was becoming clearer, his perception of people was, too. He knew he had to ask forgiveness from his ex-wife for the way he had treated her and poisoned her thoughts to agree with his own selfish lifestyle.

He understood how God, who was willing to walk that distance with others, had created him and had come near to him. Beit was going to leave behind his indifference, anger, and hatred; he was now going to live his life full of love, forgiveness, and peace. He would grow his love for the unloved, nurture his compassion for the neglected, and trample every human-made barricade serving as boundary walls constructed by religion. First, he had to experience it to extend that love and forgiveness to others.

Jesus gently made his way in love into a place where he was unwelcome. When religion said that it was not the road to travel, and that past hurts called for an alternate route, God's love paved the path in a brand-new way. Jesus undertook an adventurous trip that would bring every lost person to fellowship and relationship with the creator of the universe. When all manmade ways and human faith said it would be impossible to bridge the gap, that human beings are condemned and will remain apart from God, Jesus walked right through those falsehoods.

The truth is that Jesus, the man at the well, bridged the distance that we humans experience because of our deep hurts and because of our sin of breaking God's laws, which leave deep scars that mar our hearts and souls. He has come near to those who feel the shame and guilt of sin and pain. He has walked the distance that we have created between God and ourselves and has knocked down the walls of religious hatred, fear, and ignorance. And … he is near even when we are unaware.

Jesus wants to meet us, speak to us, and reveal his truth and himself to us. We may find him on the most unlikely roads during our life journey. He might show up at a place where we may miss him simply because he comes to us in an unexpected form. Knowing him may mean we learn to worship and view others in ways that differ from our cherished traditions or long-held beliefs. He comes very near to where our distant hearts are. He opens our eyes to see things not as they are but as reality as it ought to be, God's way.

*****

Beit walked out of his home. His next steps would take him to where he had left his woman; he wanted to ask forgiveness for everything he had done wrong. He wanted a new beginning. As he pulled the door shut behind him, he heard a knock at the front gate. As he opened the gate, he was shocked to see the two men who were standing there. They had been present when he had the mysterious encounter with the man at the well. They said they wanted to share something very interesting that had happened to them and requested a few minutes with him. They sat down in the courtyard overlooking the old city, and Beit was ready to hear what they had to say.

In the following chapter, we will hear the story that drastically changed yet another life.

Chapter 4
Religion to Worship

"Woman," Jesus replied, "believe me, a time is coming when you will worship the Father neither on this mountain nor in Jerusalem. You Samaritans worship what you do not know; we worship what we do know, for salvation is from the Jews. Yet a time is coming and has now come when the **true worshipers will worship the Father in the Spirit and in truth,** *for they are the kind of worshipers the Father seeks. God is Spirit, and his worshipers must worship in the Spirit and in truth."* (John 4:21-24).

Priest Gimel's Story

Gimel came from a long line of priests; in fact, his father and his grandfather were priests at a well-known temple in the mountains above the town. For years they offered spiritual leadership to a large community of believers. Gimel's mother always chuckled that the family had been involved in so many religious events that she almost gave birth to Gimel in the temple because her labor pains started during one of the religious ceremonies!

Even as a boy, Gimel was very involved in everything that went on in and around the temple, but the real confirmation of his calling came when he was only 12 years old. He remembers the details of that night as if they had happened just yesterday. He had finished his temple duties and was about to go to sleep when he heard the audible voice of God calling him and leading him to a mountain top. That's all he remembered when he opened his eyes. Then he ran to his grandfather, who was the priest at the time, and told him everything that had occurred. Before daybreak, the whole village knew that Gimel would be the future chosen successor priest of the people.

Soon people started coming to him for special blessings and respected him as one elected by the divine. He enjoyed every moment of being at the service of the people; he devoted long hours to studying the various ancient Scriptures. He would wake up very early and spend hours in preparation for the temple rituals. He was accustomed to many religious activities and was frequently called upon to perform official duties in the temple. His life became focused on the temple and religion; there was no time left for anything else — or anyone else.

Since he was the most eligible and religious bachelor in town, his name was often mentioned by village elders at the dinner tables of prospective young women. There were many good potential partners from various quarters of society, but when the time came, young Gimel stunned everyone. Being a spiritual man, he wanted to do something kind and charitable, so he married an ordinary woman from a very humble background. No one in the village thought he would marry a woman from Sychar, a woman of questionable repute. There were even rumors that she had been married twice before and had not been faithful to her previous husbands. But Gimel was sure that this marriage was a call from God. He had met the woman only once in the temple in the early hours of the morning while offering prayers. He inquired about her and learned that she was a poor woman who lived with her old father. He decided to help the family by marrying her and setting a good example for the community.

The wedding itself was a small and private ceremony, although he made sure that every religious requirement was met, including the custom of feeding a special meal to every orphan child of the village at the reception. He built his family on a very pious foundation. His new bride had previously gone through some tough challenges, and at last she felt religion was the answer to her problems. Now she and her husband would lead a life pleasing to God and to the townspeople.

She looked happy, and as the years went on, in addition to her other children from previous marriages, she gave birth to a beautiful daughter. Gimel wanted a son to carry on his name and his legacy and to keep the family's religious stature intact. Many in the village knew that the priest was very disappointed that his new wife had not given him the son he desperately wanted. His preference for a boy child over a girl was mainly due to a misinterpretation of an old sacred text that said gods are pleased in the worship of a man over a woman. Having a newborn should have been a joyous time, but soon the mother felt the brunt of being neglected by her husband and being burdened with too many sacred duties that were thrust upon her. She even looked a bit drawn and weary due to the daily requirements and appointments expected of her. Even the slightest mistake regarding a religious obligation was met with harsh words and severe punishment from her husband.

Once, she failed to go to Mount Gerizim for a religious holy day, and the castigation was for her to fast from food for three days as atonement. At the time, she was still weak from recently giving birth. Fasting taxed her body and embittered her spirit. All the rules were becoming too much for her. Everything that her husband did and lived for was based on religion, and there was no break or life outside it. Life had to be lived perfectly per the religious guidelines; any mistake would bring down the curse of God and punishment from man.

Abiding by all the rules and rigors broke her soul and caused her to live in fear and confusion. She wasn't sure if this type of life was truly what God wanted from her, or if this was the type of worship that pleased God. Was she being true to God, or was she just following man-made forms of control and manipulation? The last straw was when her husband, the priest, was called in by the village council members who had a very serious complaint. His wife had violated the sacred temple rules. During her monthly period, she had mistakenly touched some of the religious offerings, making them impure. The council decided that the appropriate punishment would be for her to live in the servants' quarters of her home and to relinquish the status of being married to the priest for three months.

She could not bear this treatment anymore; she was embarrassed, insulted, and in emotional and spiritual pain. The only freedom she had was when she could walk away from all the religious trappings and go to the village well to be alone. She had to get away from the religious authorities and her overbearing husband. She discovered that being alone near the well during the noontime hour was the perfect way to cope with her stress. She knew she would not be able to continue in her marriage, but she didn't know how to deal or what to do. All she knew was that the more she spent time at the well, the more she was at peace.

One day, stressed by everything that was happening and aware that she had failed her religious husband, she did what she did best: she went to the well with her water jar. She did not know that this day was going to be different. As she walked closer, she was surprised to see a man sitting by the well who appeared to be a religious figure. This was the last type of person she wanted to see that day. She didn't want any religious zealot harassing her even more than she was already harassed — especially a Jew who had beliefs so different from her own. Perhaps because she was a woman and he looked like a Pharisee, he would not even look at her, as it was against his law. Thus, she would be left undisturbed by his self-righteousness.

But that was not true; in fact, just the opposite happened. The man looked at her and smiled and instead of appearing pious or acting religious, he made a very human request: he asked her for a drink. Her life experience had taught her that religion had no place for mercy, neither does it seek it, so she was puzzled to know why this person of a different faith was so kind in his approach, very unlike her past encounters with religious people. She moved a few steps forward to have a closer look at this stranger…and at that moment she was reminded of the burning bush where one of her forefathers took a step closer to look at the phenomenon. Though she wanted to break free of the religious customs that had been burdening her for so long, she didn't want to appear non-religious at this moment; after all, she was married to a priest.

She found this Pharisee to be very different; everything he did and said was non-religious, yet he was very spiritual and exuded a personal intimacy with God. She felt like unloading onto him all the fears and struggles she was going through — all the religious torture she had endured because of the rigid standards she failed to meet. She asked him about everything that had been bothering and burdening her for so long. She wanted to know how she could be religious enough to please God. She also wanted to know about the temple, its customs, its practices, and more (even though she hated it all).

Then she heard something revelatory: the stranger told her that God is a Spirit. Then her earth shook when he explained: "You cannot please God by being religious; the Father is seeking true worshipers, not the religious folks."

For the first time, she could see the difference between practicing religion to seek God versus becoming a worshipper whom God is seeking. The man said that worship had to be offered in spirit and in truth and not bound in tradition. For the first time in her life, all her fears were relieved, and her confusion was gone. She felt like she had been set free. She didn't have to perform, she didn't have to get her actions right. It was his righteousness that made her right. His grace was sufficient in all her weakness. She didn't have to offer things and do things to please God. God was already pleased with her and that was why he offered his only begotten Son: to accept her.

This truth he was speaking was too much for her to contain and accept, and it ran counter to all she had heard from her religious leaders or religious gatherings. She suddenly began to realize that having a relationship with God was all about her *heart*, a *heart* that had to be set right with *him* before her *hands* could do any meaningful work. She felt like she was falling in love with the God of creation for the very first time. She felt like a child reaching out toward the firm hands of her heavenly Father who was there to hold her and walk with her. All the burdens of religious traditions were breaking away, and she was being delivered of all that had bound her for so long. She closed her eyes and whispered out loud, "My chains are gone, I am set free." At that moment, she felt her soul being cleansed of all the past pain and damage that religion, people, and the system had brought upon her. There was a new song in her heart and a new smile on her face.

She could not believe that God was seeking people just like her, and that they didn't have to work hard to find him. She had finally met the God who would forgive, instead of condemn or judge. Her fear of being cursed or punished vanished. She saw herself bathing in the water that was the grace of God.

She remembered the temple and the people who always came to Mount Gerizim on high holy days, to practice prayer and piety, but who returned home with heavy hearts and without feeling that God was ever truly pleased. The water jar that she was holding symbolized all the religious questions she had which were answered that day at the well. Thus, she dropped the water jar down to the ground because she didn't need it anymore. She could feel lightness encompass her spirit.

Then she ran to the village. She knew that when she arrived the afternoon prayers would be going on at the temple, and she might run into a few people who had been harsh to her in the past. It didn't matter to her now; she would tell them the news that God is seeking worshipers — not religious traditions and surface prayers. She would tell them what the man had explained to her: "God is a Spirit, so people do not have to be in a particular location to worship him." As she was running to the village to share the news, she didn't even think to look back at the well and the water jar that she had left behind.

Gimel, the Third Husband

It wasn't normal for worshipers to leave the temple before the benediction was pronounced. But today that's what happened. To his utter disbelief, the third husband, Gimel, like the first two husbands, followed the crowd going to the well. He too had heard his ex-wife sharing her testimony about how her life had been changed by the rabbi who she had met at Jacob's well. The third husband also stood motionless, his eyes fixed on the water jar.

That day, as he stood by the well, the third ex-husband clearly saw how much his life choices had negatively affected others, especially his family. In his pursuit of trying to please God, he had hurt many whom God had brought into his life. He was a man who had been so focused on religion that he had forgotten how to be a compassionate human being and how to treat his wife and family with love and respect.

His motives were pure, but his methods were corrupt; he had overlooked the important lesson about loving his neighbor and household (see Leviticus 19:18). There was no mercy in any of his religious actions. Everything he did as a holy man he did in order to fulfill the law and its requirements. That was all that mattered to him. There was no end to his hard work, and there was no place for others to make mistakes. His life was so enmeshed in the activities of the temple that he had fallen out of touch with the needs, pain, and suffering of God's people. He was far from God.

Standing there by the well that day, the third husband suddenly understood how he had become so "heavenly-minded but of no earthly good." Today, he followed the crowd to that place because he had been feeling disconnected and dissatisfied with his life ever since his wife left him. He now understood that he had chosen sacrifice over mercy concerning his family. Looking back, he saw that he was guilty of being legalistic rather than being kind — and kindness was true religion. He had driven his wife away.

Politically, he had supported the council that had implemented strict religious laws that especially burdened the poor and the marginalized people of the society. He was often the primary witness of those who were beaten with canes and those who were stoned due to serious religious sacrilege. But today something strange happened; he was tired of the religious burden he was carrying, with all its endless temple routines, ceremonies, and chants. He knew in his heart that all of it had made him a bitter person.

For the first time he prayed, "God, if you are real, please show yourself." But he didn't know that God had a strange sense of humor. When he opened his eyes after praying, he saw his estranged wife standing right outside the temple. She looked serene, not her usual bitter, madwoman appearance. She was smiling at him! And she didn't have her water jar with her, the jar that represented her liberal attitude that threatened everything he stood for. But today he knew she was not there to argue but, rather, to tell him about someone who had changed her life.

Her third husband, Gimel, the temple priest, walked over to her, and she immediately started sharing everything that had happened at the well. Then she invited him and the temple Senate to come and meet this man. When they arrived at the well, Gimel was taken aback at the sight of a Jewish rabbi. This was not what he was expecting to see. He knew his ex-wife was completely against everything religious, so he couldn't believe that she had led them to see a rabbi! It was difficult for him to absorb and his first impulse was to turn around and leave. But he too wanted that peace and joy beaming from her face. He couldn't resist it and wanted to see the reason for it with his own eyes.

As he stepped closer, he could see the water jar sitting beside the well, the jar that she always carried with her. She didn't cling to it anymore as a security blanket. Now she was confident, satisfied, and able to live life in whatever form she found it. Even though his religiosity kept invading his mind, telling him to move him away from the teacher, he could not ignore what he saw in his ex-wife that he desperately needed himself. He knew he had become a difficult person to live with and an angry person within. All his religious lifestyle had done was alienate him. It did not and could not save him. He needed something more, and maybe this stranger was the key.

As the crowd followed the teacher into the city, Gimel was still standing by the well, staring at the water jar, along with a few other men. They waited there until everyone was out of sight, and then as a group they slowly made their way toward the place where the teacher was staying for the night. The third husband wanted to know what was so special about the teacher, the secret to his ex-wife's transformation. He knew very well that religion was not the answer. Everything he had chased after had destroyed him and his family. He wanted a fresh start.

Just then he heard the teacher talk about the fresh, living water that he would give to all who came to him and asked. Being a priest, the only thing the third husband had ever known was to ask his parishioners to drink the holy water that his temple provided (and he knew that water would soon dry out without bringing transformation). So, he moved a bit closer to the Jewish teacher to hear him better. Gimel was careful to write down what he heard that night onto the temple scroll he was carrying in his hands. The crowd that came to listen to the teacher thinned as the night darkened, but he stayed because he wanted to learn everything he could.

Religion Is Outward; Worship Is Internal

This third husband, the well-known priest, was shocked to hear that religion is outward and worship is internal. All his adult life had been consumed with trying to make everything look good externally. He didn't care about cleaning up the mess that had accumulated inside him. If everything on the exterior was clean and per tradition it was all right with him. When he heard that the cup must be clean from the inside first to be used by the master, he couldn't hold back his tears. He felt broken and like everything that he had been holding within him for so long was leaking out. Wiping tears from his face, he knew the changes that he was trying to make externally would always be limited by his behavior if there was no change in his spirit. He wanted lasting change, and that meant creating a space within him where God could reside and build his kingdom. The third husband wanted to allow this Spirit to quench his deepest thirst first, so that the life of living water could flow through him and bless others. It was a life-changing lesson, and he inscribed it neatly onto the scroll.

The Spirit of God

He stopped writing to reflect more on what he heard the teacher say: good works or good deeds cannot make our spirits come alive. We need a spiritual rebirth to become people who please God. Our actions, however noble, are like a wrinkled piece of cloth that has no value; only the Spirit of God can bring a spiritually dead person back to abundant, glorious life. What the rabbi Jesus said helped Gimel understand: only those who are spiritually alive can please God or do his work.

So, everything religious the third husband had been doing at the temple was in the flesh and that was the reason he felt so burdened and burned out. He needed the Spirit the teacher was talking about — the Spirit that is poured out upon all those who believe and seek him. The third husband wanted to live a peaceful and meaningful life. He now knew that while our minds and our bodies play important roles, it is only in the Spirit that people can understand and know God truly. God is a Spirit, and every human, wherever and whoever they are, can connect with him and receive the Spirit of life from him. It is the Holy Spirit who renews anyone who is tired of *doing* things, and it is the Holy Spirit who shapes them into the people God wants them to become.

Religious Work Brings Death; Spiritual Work Brings Life

The third husband finally received the answer he was seeking to a long-standing question: "How could I, being so religious and following all the traditions, still have caused so much pain and grief to my family?" The teacher explained how all our religious efforts, when grounded in self, only bring death in our relationships. They make us self-righteous and judgmental because, without us realizing it, our focus is on the perceptions of others, instead of on ourselves. On the other hand, spiritually alive people have died to the world's definition of living, and now live per the Spirit living within them. Gimel, with the written pages in his hand, went out to find someone with whom he could share his heart. He was led to a strange home hidden among the upper hills of the village. He stood before a gate, took a breath and then knocked. When the door opened, he walked in to find a few men gathered around a fire. He sat with them. He heard one man sharing about how he was lost for a long time and that was how, oddly, he actually found himself.

In the next chapter, we will hear this story told in that men's gathering. A story that also involved an unnamed woman and a strange man.

James Levi

Chapter 5
Prophet to Messiah

"My food," said Jesus, *"is to do the will of Him who sent me and to finish His work. Don't you have a saying, 'It's still four months until harvest'? I tell you, open your eyes and look at the fields! They are ripe for harvest. Even now the one who reaps draws a wage and harvests a crop for eternal life, so that the sower and the reaper may be glad together. Thus, the saying 'One sows and another reaps' is true. I sent you to reap what you have not worked for. Others have done the hard work, and you have reaped the benefits of their labor."* (John 4:34-38)

Dalet, the Fourth Husband

Dalet was known by some as the medicine-man, but for others he was the village healer. The village, where he lived with his wife, the unnamed woman, was not far from Sychar. For a very long time the couple wanted to have a child but to no avail. It was not that they couldn't conceive; the problem was that none of her pregnancies lasted more than a few weeks. Whenever she got pregnant there was rejoicing in the village, and then suddenly there was a sharp pain that resulted in a miscarriage. Losing their unborn babies had caused insurmountable emotional pain for them. Some villagers called it a curse, but Dalet believed in his medicine and trusted it would work one day.

Though many from other villages, and even people from Sychar, often sought help from this village healer, when it came to curing his own wife, he had failed. His wife said that they should seek the help from a spiritual healer and not rely on his medicine. Dalet refused to accept her suggestion because he felt strongly that the cure was in finding the right mixture of herbs. But his wife, after suffering the trauma of losing so many babies, had found hope and peace among her ancestral devotions. Dalet felt that she was on a dangerous path because she didn't pay attention to his opinions or views. She would often disappear into the woods for many days and some even saw her cry at the village well. But whenever Dalet bought up that issue, she would say that she had gone to speak with the prophets. And every time she left, she always had the water jar with her, a sign that she was at the well. That was strange to a man who believed only in the practical science of medicine, who spent most of this time finding cures for village illnesses and creating new herbal mixtures that helped his growing practice and queue of patients.

The Samaritan woman had also, because of her past, found a way to cope with life and live with loss. The painful memories of failed marriages were a heavy burden to carry. The best way to get through each day was to avoid facing her true self, her fears, and the demons that haunted her. She would do that by taking her water jar to the well, the place that had become her escape. In moments of desperation and weakness, she would go to the well. She would lower her water jar with her rope and be reminded of the words of her forefather Jacob, a prophet, who had blessed his descendants by saying, "You will be a fruitful bough by a well; your branches will run over the wall." These words comforted her soul when she felt surrounded by the walls of hatred, failure, and pain. As the water jar touched the water in the well, her spirit touched heavenly spirits and would often be revived by the felt presence of the prophets from the past. These experiences would comfort her heart and give her the strength and will to come back to the well daily.

Then this afternoon something unusual happened, there weren't any clouds in the sky. Usually, clouds rose high up from the Kinneret Sea because of the humid climate, but today there were none. As she neared the well, her steps quickened, and her heart began to beat faster. She knew her thirst would be quenched in a moment. Her mind started to run faster than her body and for a moment she felt lifted out of her skin and in the strange company of prophets. Then suddenly she froze, her feet too heavy to move even an inch further. Her mind and eyes were locked in dismay at the sight of an unknown stranger at her well. She was so upset that she felt tears forming in her eyes.

The presence of this man disturbed her, but she was so hot from the scorching day that she decided to ignore him and continue with her routine of fetching a cool drink of water. But then the stranger spoke to her directly, seeking a conversation with her, when all everyone else had done was wrote her off. His gentle voice spoke words that sounded greater than any words uttered by her prophets. All her beliefs about her faith began to crumble. She didn't want this to be happening to her, she couldn't bear to hear anything unlike what her forefathers had taught her people. But what she was feeling in the presence of this man and the words she was hearing from him hit her like a hurricane threatening everything she knew. She thought of standing up against him, although she knew she didn't have any strength that could compete with his force. She hoped within herself that perhaps her prophets could help her, so she mustered her courage and asked him, "Are you greater than our father Jacob?" There was a silence, no argument, but a gentle offer: "I will give you living water." She understood that he was not talking about the water that came from the well that was given by Jacob to his son Joseph. It was a very personal offer...something which was special and unique for her. She couldn't resist that offer. In that moment, came a fuller understanding. She wasn't prepared for any of it, although someone had been prepared long before and was waiting on her behalf.

This was different and far better than anything the prophets had ever promised. This was not just something that simply felt a bit good on the outside; this truth touched her innermost heart and she felt the fountain of living water springing forth from within her very being. She was filled with joy, and she could laugh again after a long time of sadness. Living life as a failure was too heavy for her, but now she didn't have to face her tomorrow alone.

This realization changed everything, and she couldn't keep it to herself. She ran to the village and shared this good news with those who were on a similar journey — seeking yet not finding the true meaning of their lives. She was now able to relate to them in a new way because she had been where they are, and she didn't want them to stay there any longer. They wanted what she had received and were willing to follow her wherever she wanted to take them. They were willing to do anything and everything to have what the rabbi Jesus gave her.

At the Well

At times, the unnamed woman claimed that she heard voices from the prophets. In those moments, she found rest, but at other times she would hear voices that agitated and disturbed her. Some village folks said that she was losing her mind. But she knew she wasn't insane. She was convinced her frequent visits to the well were keeping her mental health in check.

One afternoon she met someone who was wiser, more powerful, and more loving than all the religious Pharisees she had previously encountered. Today, she had met the totality of what all the other prophets had tried to explain but couldn't. Today she had met the living and breathing subject of their prophecies, and there was no longer a need for her to seek any more answers. She had been told that one day a real teacher would appear, the one they call the Messiah, and he would explain everything. But she didn't know that he would come to ease her suffering and that he would give her the drink that would take away the pain in her life. This was a true deliverance; a miraculous meeting with the one who was thought to be in the remote future yet was invading her ordinary now. The king of the universe had waited for her at the well and met her just as she was, vulnerable, her fears, pain, and suffering exposed. The rabbi, who indeed was the Messiah the world was waiting for, considered that tender meeting with an ordinary woman in her ordinary moment, glorious.

Dalet, the fourth husband, stood looking at the water jar and acknowledged to himself that he had often let his wife down when she needed him. He knew they had drifted apart, each retreating into their own pain because of the loss of their babies, never seeking each other's help to heal together. He realized that, for the most part, his community had been unaware of the pain and suffering that they had gone through as a married couple. Today he stood silent, at a loss for words, knowing that his wife had finally found something that she had been seeking for a long time. The rabbi filled her with living, flowing, refreshing water from the fountain of eternal life.

This woman returned to the well every day to satisfy her physical need for water, but today she left that place without her jar and without even thinking about being thirsty again. Her spiritual thirst had been satisfied with everlasting, living water from God's fountain of life. The one who sat at Jacob's well was the one Jacob had bowed down to when he could not win the wrestling match by Jabbok's brook. She had found the Savior, the Messiah, the one the prophets had spoken of but never met, the one Jacob preached about but never saw. Now she met the one who was greater and this one was there to fill her with his good news of love and mercy and grace.

After she received rabbi Jesus, the Messiah, she knew she had to run and tell others trying to find hope and consolation in the prophets. She ran to tell those who had been hurt and who had hurt people; she ran to everyone she knew who needed to meet the one she had just met, the Savior of the world. The one she now knew was the promised one.

She had to tell her people that they couldn't miss hearing what he had to say and that they didn't have to wait any longer for the Messiah. They could just come exactly as they were and meet him at the well and be healed, delivered, and accepted by him as the fulfillment of all the prophecies. She ran toward the village and in her rush left her water jar behind.

A Healer Needing a Healer:
Dalet had been busy formulating a new medicine that he hoped would heal his wife's inability to carry a child to full term. He was also working on a cure for people with anxiety, though he knew through his personal experience that it could not work as well as his patients hoped. He was frustrated because he couldn't help more people, and in that admission of failure he

remembered his wife whom he had lost. Now, as she ran into the village, he called out to her. She greeted him, and they talked about the rabbi she had just met. Something began to stir deep within him as they spoke. As he examined himself, he understood how foolish it had been for him to believe that his medicinal cures and potions could cure people of their inner pain and free them from spiritual trauma. It was in this state of confusion that he decided to go to the well along with the crowd that his wife was leading. And there for the first time, the fourth husband, who had only believed in medicine and herbal cures, came face to face with something deeper and more real. Today he found a new healing power flowing from this stranger — the one who talked about healing the soul. He was the one who would die and set all mankind free from the curse of sin.

For much of his life, Dalet, in his attempt to heal human pain and suffering via his medical treatments, had refused to believe in sin and the curse. All he knew about were diseases and illnesses and ways to cure them, but he never understood that sin was the cause of people's pain and suffering and the world's woes. Before that day, he had never known that the remedy for spiritual illness is to turn one's life and limb over to the healer — Jesus, the Son of God. He had never known that for him and his patients to be completely healed, a sinless

Savior would have to pay a price, a Savior that would die so that he and his people could live.

Dalet, the fourth husband, could not believe it at first, but slowly he felt relief that he now knew the truth. He also felt sorrow for how he failed his wife and other people, people he had promised to cure. There was clear proof that what this man was speaking was true — he saw with his own eyes that his wife was now on the path to recovery from all the depression, anger, and loneliness she had been suffering with for years. She was standing there facing the crowd, willing to be vulnerable about what she had gone through. She shared her life story, she talked about her pain, and she told the crowd that they didn't have to wait for the Savior to come — he was with them at that very moment. The fourth husband saw her compassion for the people and knew that the Messiah had set her free.

Dalet, her fourth husband and the village healer, needed a healer himself. He needed a new understanding of truth that would change his life and the lives of all who would listen. As he listened to the rabbi, he started writing everything down on the back of the medical research papers he had with him. This is what he wrote:

Pain is Deeper:

Pain is much deeper than what I see in my sick patients. There are many who do not have any physical illness but are suffering from emotional, psychological, and mental traumas. What I see in this rabbi's treatment of others is that he is very present with those in pain. He can sit with a person who has been suffering for a long time. When I, along with my community, had abandoned my wife, Jesus took time for her. He was willing to include her in his plan, to come and meet and listen to her. He did not tell her a lot of things, but for the first time in her life he was there to listen. The rabbi acknowledged her pain and identified with her. I understand now that I have failed in being there for her because of how I left her while I was seeking the cure for her inability to carry a child to full term. But I never bothered to find out how she was feeling or what she really was looking for in her time of pain. In the past, my eyes were open only to external wounds and symptoms; I didn't see what my wife was experiencing within her spirit. I didn't take time to see what she was going through.

Pain Heals a Community:

Many times, I got so caught up in healing others and being a healer that I forgot that I need healing as well. My escape route was to be more involved in taking care of those suffering and in that, somehow, I numbed my own pain. But that doesn't help today as I stand with others who are in the same place as I am: broken. Being able to be open with my wounds allows me to start the process towards my healing. I can see how my wife was changed and restored because of someone who was willing to stop for her and allowed her to be transparent about her own pain. I am willing to share my brokenness and my pain in that group and am willing to share with other men who are also experiencing similar pain.

Dalet's writing started to fill up the pages but he couldn't stop, even though his hand hurt. He paused for a moment, turned what he was learning over in his mind and wrote some more:

The Soul-Healer, the Messiah:
I hear how this rabbi is not just a prophet, but he is the fulfillment of all prophecies. He is the one who was promised to come to restore everything to its original state. I started to remember my school days, when I had been trained under my mentor. I had often heard how things were once right and perfect. Everything was in order, but then human beings, with their greed and rebellion, had destroyed God's perfect world by inviting chaos and suffering. In my practice, I know that my medicine did not completely solve patients' problems but, rather, just minimized their symptoms. Often my patients

came back with the same illness and sometimes with an even more severe condition. Now I understand that there is something that will completely cure humans of their suffering. Now I know someone who had to pay a price for all the wrong that had been done by humans. Now I know that none of us can pay that price. I heard how the rabbi was not just a human being but was also the one who had come to die for the wrongdoings of human beings. He was the Savior, the Messiah who would heal humanity from all its wickedness and selfishness and the resulting suffering. I know there is a better place where people can live in peace and harmony, rather than just experiencing suffering forever. There is a new understanding that is settling in my mind and a peace that is calming my spirit. Some clarity is coming to me about how to comfort my patients, those who have suffered because of sickness and death of their loved ones. I now know how to be present with those who are in pain and feel peace about how everything can be set right once again. There is someone greater than all the prophets. He is the Savior that the world had been waiting for and now he was here, and I recognized him.

Dalet's tears were rolling down and dampening his tunic, but he felt the warmth of those men around him. They came and placed their hands on his shoulders and, in their silence, supported him. There was a long pause, then one more person spoke up.

In the next chapter, we will hear one more story from still another man.

Chapter 6
Man to Husband

"Just then His disciples returned and were surprised to find Him talking with a woman. But no one asked, 'What do you want?' or 'Why are you talking with her?' (John 4:27)

Hei, the Fifth Husband

Hei, the fifth husband, walked close to the well; he was the quietest of the group and the least emotional. Unlike the other four men, he was withdrawn and world-weary. Hei didn't seem to belong; it was as if he was ashamed to be there. He didn't even have the strength to lift up his face. Hei was a man who had never wanted to grow up. At a very early age he inherited vast wealth from his deceased father, who was known to be a very rich man who owned many heads of cattle and farms across the land. He hired many servants who would look after his various properties. But the sudden death of his father meant Hei took over the business at an early age. He soon learned the reins of business — as well as an immoral life that wealth brought with it. He was known to travel around to his various farms doing business and pleasure simultaneously. Throughout his life he had indulged in selfish, egocentric gratifications. He didn't care how his actions affected others in his world. The only things that mattered to him were his own desires, and the only people who mattered were those who would help him fulfill them. He would go to any extent to get what he wanted. He didn't care what price others had to pay for the suffering he brought upon them — like his several children who never knew their father or the wives he had abandoned. They didn't matter to him.

Many say Hei, the fifth husband, was living and reliving his teenage years with everything centered on fulfilling his youthful impulses. He would spend his days wasting away in the company of folk singers, drinking and making melody (a hidden passion) in a heart that many thoughts was cold, dark, and sorrowful. In the process, he caused a lot of pain to a lot of people. But nothing seemed to bother him on the surface because he was deeply addicted to sensual pleasures, drinking, and wild parties. Forgetting his problems was all he cared about, and his questionable so-called friends were happy to keep him squarely on his destructive path. His latest wife from Samaria was left alone to fend for their son. The fifth husband as a man simply refused to be a husband or father and would not take responsibility to carry out his family duties.

His wife suffered so much that she also started living a compromised life; she didn't care to keep the promise of fidelity she made at their wedding. This ultimately brought her more pain and suffering. Her loneliness drove her to a life of isolation and escaping the world and that often meant to be near the well, all by herself, cut off from everyone and even sometimes from her.

This Samaritan woman at the well wanted to escape her life of rejection and suffering, and she wanted to get away from her husband who had refused to grow up and be responsible. In a vengeful moment, she thought that being with other men might win her husband back or maybe help her feel complete or accepted. But most of these illicit relationships were worse than being with her own husband. She ended up wasting her time with immature men who were harsh, insensitive, or even physically abusive to her.

Today she was desperate to go to her favorite place to be alone and escape the pain. At the well she could forget how deeply she had been hurt by all the men in her life. She went to the well expecting some momentary relief. But then she saw a man sitting by the well resting, and then he asked her to give him a drink. Suddenly she felt the pain of her past rising within her, anger simmering to a boil. She immediately assumed that she was once again being used, and she braced herself to be abused again. The only way she knew how to fight back was to go on the offensive. She wanted to make sure that this man (who was probably like all other men and only interested in her for his own pleasure) would get to see the wrong side of her. So she was prepared to fight back and make sure that he (and every other man) would never hurt her again.

She had been hurt too many times by men and by her foolish husbands, and today she wasn't going to bear it anymore. She also knew how her own attempts to rectify things had turned against her and caused her additional pain and suffering. As she prepared to fight this stranger who had trespassed her sacred territory, she treaded carefully. She paused to observe him closely. She felt all her anger and crazy thoughts slowly easing. She noticed that the man was different from all the other men she had met. What shocked her was how she was respected and graciously treated by a total stranger, a Jewish man, a rabbi. In that moment, everything stood still. All her life she was used and sexually abused by men who didn't care for her. Though she carried that pain, today in that place somehow it didn't feel burdensome — it felt lifted.

This stranger was not interested in what he could get from her, but rather he was there to help her and give her everything she ever needed. He was not there to hurt her, but rather to take away the hurt that she had been carrying for so long. He was not there to make her cry, but rather to wipe away the tears that had been untouched by a caring hand for years. For the first time, she met a man who didn't act like a boy. Rather, he showed her what a real man looked like, a caring, kind, and gentle person. A man who wanted to protect her and make sure she knew that she was loved, heard, and comforted.

*****

Hei, the fifth husband, now standing all alone, slowly found enough courage to take those baby steps toward the well; he looked closely at the water jar left nearby. His mind replayed various scenes of the past, and he understood how his actions, his selfish lifestyle, and his immaturity hurt all the women in his life. His refusal to grow up and to own his actions resulted in hurting many poor young women and children who had lost their chance to live decent lives.

Feeling ashamed, he tried to focus his thoughts on the rabbi. He was at the well because he had followed his friend. He had taken refuge at his friend's place, the only house open to him. He had suffered a major health crisis that caused him to lose all this wealth and most of his friends. He hit rock bottom, and everyone deserted him; he lost everything in what seemed like a mere second and he was empty inside and out. This friend was the only one who stuck with him; all the others had walked away when he lost his fame, fortune, and lavish lifestyle. His one and only friend was following a woman who said there was a rabbi at the well — someone they all should meet. The fifth husband had no idea what he would find at the well.

As they approached the well he saw the water jar — a symbol of his wife's isolation and his rebellion and stunted growth. He listened to the rabbi and when he rose to walk into the village, the fifth husband walked along and seated himself with others who wanted to hear what Jesus had to say. Then, as his gaze turned to the woman who had led the crowd to the well earlier in the day, Hei was startled to see that he was looking at one of his ex-wives. He never saw her quite like the way she looked today. She was beautiful, happy, humble, and full of peace. What touched him so deeply was the way this woman described the man, the teacher. She acknowledged before everyone that the rabbi understood and respected her and gave her the time, the value, and the dignity that she felt she rightfully deserved. And she was right. Perhaps this was the first time Hei opened his mind to understand her rather than try to make everyone else understand him.

The fifth husband wanted to hear everything being said and was grateful for his friend who not only gave him a place to live but brought him to place where he could now live differently. He felt within his spirit that he was in that place that he had been seeking for so long. For the first time, he knew he had been lost and realized that he was now found — to live in service of others rather than solely for himself. He took out a small notebook from his pocket that was filled with songs he had composed over the years, songs that he penned when he felt lonely. Now, Hei started writing descriptions of this man who he found to both be out of this world yet perfectly fit into his world. He took notes as well as he could.

He Waited for Her

Unlike other men who didn't care if she was kept waiting, rabbi Jesus was different. He took time out from the busyness of his life and kept other distractions aside (even sending his disciples away) and waited for her. He made her feel special. He was a true gentleman. He didn't force her to meet him at a place where he was comfortable. Rather, he met her where she was comfortable. It was her timing and her questions (not his) that were important. He respected her by being there for her. In this way, rabbi Jesus's encounter with this woman showed the character of God and how he deals with humanity.

When we are affected by separation, with the burden of wrong and guilt of sin weighing heavy on us, God meets us on our territory and makes time for us. He became a human so that we could understand that God is not unfamiliar with our suffering and pain and the temptations we face. The Samaritan woman represents each of us, caught up in our own world of sin and shame, hiding from ourselves and from our own people — and most of all running from the very God who created us.

We all hold on to our own water jars and try to find meaning and purpose in our lives. Some of us get meaning out of our work, some create pride in our achievements or family, and some of us are broken and admit that nothing can hold us together. We are as empty as the water jar and must keep coming back to the same well. Even if we think it is a safe place, our security, peace, and manufactured relief do not last. Only when we accept the One who comes to meet us, makes time for us, and longs to quench our deepest thirst and reestablish our broken relationships will we experience abundant, living-watered life.

He Asked of Her

The manliness of Jesus is manifested in his humanness, his weakness, his need, and in his asking. One who is in need and is asking for a drink because he is tired appears weak in a culture where a man is esteemed for being self-made and self-reliant. By society's standards, being a man means being in charge, having all the answers, and not needing to ask for anything. Suffering silently rather than hurt one's ego. Rabbi Jesus Christ, being God of the universe, is the creator who made the waters of the ocean and the skies above. Yet he preferred to empower the woman in that moment. He didn't seize the moment for his own glory. He was there to talk to her, ask for her assistance, and show her how valuable she was, that she could serve even the king of kings. When no other man valued her, this king chose her to be the one to give him a drink, a powerful appointment which none could understand, not even her.

Rabbi Jesus was there to offer the woman a gift. He came there to meet her and give her a sense of worth, of self-value, and ultimately to offer her eternal peace and joy. His giving was through his asking. It was a perfect picture of God, who came into the world as a baby born in a manger, in a vulnerable and weak position, whose parents begged for a room in the village inn of Bethlehem but found a humble manger on the outskirts of the city. Instead of being born into a palace, he chose a barn. Instead of being born of a wealthy, cosmopolitan woman, he asked a peasant virgin teenager to allow him to rent her womb to enter the world through her. The man of God, the chosen of heaven, came asking and is still asking any who will listen today if they want to accept the gift of living waters that will change their lives forever.

The fifth husband's note cards were filling up as fast as the tears in his eyes. He kept writing because his heart was moved, and it felt warm after such a long time of being stone cold. For years, he had not felt anything; his lifestyle of emptiness had cost a heavy price on his body, spirit and soul. His remedy for numbing his aching heart was drinking hard and wild partying and that had made him cold and immovable. But now a fresh wave of love came sweeping in like a hurricane, and he felt as if he had been born once again in the presence of this rabbi.

He Listened to Her

The woman came to the well and when she was asked for a drink by the stranger, her reaction had a lot to do with her history of hurt and pain, her story of suffering, her cultural worldview, and how she made sense of life, God, and people. The man was willing to intently listen to her; he made her feel valued and heard. He accepted her questions, her doubts, and wanted to help her handle her frustration and confusion. Her blunt attitude did not disturb him, and he didn't let her remarks affect his ego. He listened not just to her words but also listened to her heart. And for the very first time she felt honored.

The best thing Christ offers us is his compassionate listening ears; He allows us to share our heart with him and speak to him from our place of confusion, fear, and doubt. The reason Christ entered our space and time and announced the coming of the kingdom was to help us know that there is hope. He is with us through his Spirit to extend his comfort. From the very moment the unnamed woman accepted Jesus for who he was, no one ever again could use and abuse her, shut her down and out, or keep her from speaking her heart. The coming of Christ opens the way for every man, woman, and child to be heard, and every marginalized community to thrive in unity.

There was a long silence in the courtyard. The tea cups were empty and tea pots were cold. The fire was dying out, yet the

Spirit was ablaze. Then they heard a loud knock at the door. Each of them looked up.

Chapter 7

Ahni

Jesus said to her, "You are right when you say you have no husband. The fact is, you have had five husbands, and the man you now have is not your husband. What you have just said is quite true."

Ahni, the Sixth Man of Sychar

As the afternoon was moving fast into dusk, most of the crowd from the village that had accompanied the woman had disappeared. I, Ahni, the sixth man, was still at the well, along with five men from Sychar, the town in Samaria. By now, the rabbi had already left, yet his presence remained still — all of us could feel it. The six of us were feeling something new bursting forth. Never had this happened to the men of Sychar, men who had been abused, hated, bullied, and taught to hit back and be negative in words and deeds.

But the truth was that we were all hurting from within, afraid, ashamed, and angry with ourselves. We were mean, not only to our oppressors, but we were mean by nature because of generational patterns being repeated. Often our reactions were expressed harshly toward others, including our wives, who have suffered at our hands because we ourselves have been victims and turned on them as oppressors.

But today one man stepped into our world, one who was not of this world but came to heal and love this world. He came without hate or negativity, without anger or fear, and without hurt or pain. He was right there with us to heal, change hearts, and give of himself. He was there to give to us what everyone who comes into this world needs — an abundant life full of joy, peace, and love.

As I was looking at these five men who were obviously deep in thought about the day's surprising encounter with the stranger, I could see that they, like myself, were still trying to absorb all that they heard. Their appearance and expressions seemed to reveal that their lives had not turned out exactly the way they had imagined. In that moment, I felt a common bond with each of them. We had started off on the race of this life with good intentions, but before we had made it to the halfway mark, we were out of steam and feeling lost, incomplete, and like failures. Everything we thought would fill our lives left us wanting.

All the accomplishments, trophies, everything we used to value seemed meaningless and wasteful as we gazed upon the water jar. For the first time, we six men realized that our life choices and decisions had had dire consequences that damaged countless lives, ultimately impacting the community we lived in and humanity at large. Instead of becoming agents of human flourishing, our actions and selfishness had made us agents of human destruction. Instead of creating peace, we had given rise to havoc.

Our Eyes Were Opened

For the first time our eyes were opened to a new understanding. We now knew that having a right spirit and intentions were not enough to help us finish well. We hadn't realized that the environment and the system into which we belonged often worked against us. Now it was clear: the whole community can become part of a web of deception that traps innocent, good, hardworking people into a life of intolerance, self-absorption, and supposed piety.

I stood there unmoved, yet totally moved with what was happening right in front of my eyes this late afternoon. I felt my emotions churn and my inner being unfold. Then, one of the men turned toward me and looked at me with a look that can only be described as a gaze into the hidden corners of my heart. I was sensing his pain, his desire to be set free and repay everything that he had stolen — the years of nurture, cherishing, and positive encouragement and the time he could have spent building up his spouse, his children, his community. There was guilt etched all over his face. How could he ever rebuild the lives that had been shattered because of his selfishness? I could hear his silent cry, "How could I ever repay it?"

In that brief instant, I recognized the man. He was the first husband of the woman, the man who was campaigning for the town's mayoral position. Now, standing there with a dream of someday becoming a mayor, he looked and felt ashamed and empty, yet there was a faint hope in his eyes. He finally realized what really mattered in life were the personal relationships that are built over the years. Relationships over popularity. He was thinking about all the hollow public speeches he had given, never really addressing the true needs of the community — only telling the people what they wanted to hear and never following up on his promises.

By now my eyes were tearing up, and I could feel tears coursing down my cheeks. I was experiencing the same conviction this well-known man contesting for public office was feeling, and we both were unashamed to express it for the first time in a public place. Now there was no more hiding. I felt the same courage to stand up as I remembered my own shortcomings. I remembered when I was chasing popularity and public acceptance. How I wanted people to accept me for who I was and how I sought to be a people-pleaser and would do anything for recognition. I always thought that my worth came from people's praise and in the process completely forgot what God thought of me. I avoided God's words of guidance in my life and welcomed the accolades of fickle people who could turn their backs on me in the blink of an eye.

I, Ahni, remember clearly when the work I was involved in was very satisfying and meaningful. I was gaining acceptance from a community that had been longing for someone like me to assist them. I was serving the people and they were, in many ways and at various times, being helped through my work. This was confirmed by the leaders within the community, which was a seal of approval for me. I could sense that I was right in the center of the will of God, and I knew I could make even more of a difference if I could expand my work to more people who were in need.

As a spiritual figure, I would visit elderly people in senior citizen homes, meet young people on their playing fields, and tell them about God's love for them. For the first time, both young and old came to know that God cared for them right where they were. There was a lot of anticipation about what God was doing in and great expectations of what he would do in the future. In the middle of such a relevant and effective ministry, I had to make a move to a totally new location as the work came to sudden pause. It didn't make sense at all, but somehow, I followed his direction. It was a hard time and a difficult transition of leaving everything behind and moving to a place of unknown.

Reluctantly I Moved

Reluctantly, I moved the family to the new place where no one knew me. There weren't any ministry opportunities to be found. It seemed that I had lost my identity. I had been drawing my sense of worthiness from the works that I had done and the opinions of other people. But now, in this new and unfamiliar place, the joy was gone. I became an angry person who hated everything and everyone around me — and above all, I was angry at God himself.

Amid that frustration and chaos, God spoke into my life. He was asking questions that I had never wanted to deal with but, like these men from Sychar, I was forced to wrestle and ask myself, *what do I value in life?* Was it the public recognition or personal relationships? The work, the appreciation, the great feeling of being accepted by people had just been a cover-up so that I did not have to face the real me and the insecurities and fears that made me feel weak and less than the man I wanted to be. Yet God, in all his infinite knowledge, being aware of each of our thoughts, drew close to me to build a relationship, so I wouldn't feel neglected and ignored.

He drew near to me, near to my "well" of confusion, fear, shame, and anger; he left all to be with me. I could see all the me-centered things I thought would make me happy. My work and service were there to serve *me*, to achieve the goal of making *me* feel good and project *me* in the ministry, to satisfy *me* rather than to serve *God* and do what *he* wanted.

I, Ahni, that afternoon near the well, standing with the five men from Sychar, realized this was a time of introspection and a time to humble myself and find the joy that comes when we find God. It was a place of total surrender, a place to be in that awesome presence of the sacred, unashamed and full of peace.

It was a difficult road for anyone to travel. Especially for men like those from Sychar who often found our self-worth and sense of identity in our work, and our value in what people say.

The questions that gripped my heart were: *What if, in a moment, everything we do and everything people say about us is taken away? Would our world collapse, or would we still be able to have peace knowing that God is with us and pleased with us? Do we find God's favor only in the times of successful work, occupation, or acceptance?* In the stillness of my time at the well, I could sense the deep presence of the rabbi Jesus within my spirit.

I was led to remember a special time he carried me. In a time of seeking him, he opened a place for me that I never thought possible. It was a special place of service, a place where I had to once again enter a world of brokenness and pain and suffering — a place where his light had to be shone into the darkest caverns of my life. He gave me a new place of ministry among those incarcerated in the prison. It was a very difficult ministry opportunity among the people who were outcast, marginalized and daily living in pain, fear and guilt. I wasn't prepared for it, but God gave me his heart and his passion and his Spirit to help me shine his light, daily, into the shadowy recesses of the hearts and minds of those to whom I ministered.

It has become a life-changing ministry where I meet with people who are going through difficult and hopeless times in their lives, often rejected by their own, as well as struggling to forgive themselves. God opened my eyes to see him, his work, and his ministry. I am amazed and I am grateful to be able to say with mighty confidence that as we trust God and follow him, he will lead us onto the paths that take us into places where we will find — like Rabbi on the road to Sychar — lost people with hurting souls, who have given up hope. Just as Jesus touched the Samaritan woman and the town of Sychar, God will bless our work every day to make a difference within our world.

I know that God is in control and he is the one who can still make the fountain of living water run from the lives of those who accept him as God's son and our Savior. All those who are empty, who return to their various "wells" time and again, hoping to fill their water jars with water that will always leave them thirsty for more meaning and purpose, only have to allow Jesus to fill their jars with his eternal, life-giving living water and they will never again feel thirst or be empty.

As I, Ahni, was thinking about this phenomenal truth, the first man, the first husband, walked up to me and put his hands on my shoulders. He stayed close to me and in his nearness was a cry for help to walk this new path. To leave accolades for anonymity. To build personal relationships with souls that were lost, hurting, and in pain. This was a holy moment.

As I started to leave the well, I saw the second man approaching, the man who owned the bakery and wouldn't sell to people different from his own. He walked toward me, and I recalled a time when I wanted to take revenge for all the pain I suffered and the suffering of my loved ones.

My mind went back to one night when I was about to go to sleep. After I blew out the lamp on the nightstand, I gently rested my hand on my woman, the one I was living with and held it there. Instead of warmth and tenderness, she was tense, and her shoulders were stiff. I moved my hands to her face. I could feel tears in her eyes. I pulled my hands away, sat up on the side of the bed, lit the lamp, turned toward her, and started to apologize. Without knowing what was going on, I assumed the best way to help her was to ask for forgiveness, thinking that perhaps I may have caused her some pain. But my apology made her cry even more.

Then when I was quiet, she explained the situation, and I was relieved to know that I was not the cause (at least this time) for what had happened to her. I held her hands once again and gripped them firmly, indicating that I was willing to listen if she wanted to share. In my mind, I was thinking that I would take care of everything and solve any difficulty that she was facing in the village, but I learned that she was not looking for my help in that way.

I could feel her pain as she described how a friend who she was close to had wounded her with insults. I already knew about the incident because she had mentioned how this woman had demeaned her a few days earlier.

But that was not what was bothering her this night. Earlier that day the same friend had come to ask her for help in the middle of a crisis. The friend who had insulted my woman just a few weeks ago, now, without even apologizing, had the audacity to ask her for help? My anger surfaced immediately. I still remember the exact moment, under the dim light of the lamp, I looked at the innocent face of my woman and gave her the best solution I thought any man could give. I said: "Never, ever help her! You should make her pay for what she did to you and let her feel the brunt of what she does to others!"

I was as firm as I could be, and I was sure that my advice would help her. She knew that I, her man, would be there to guide her through these types of predicaments. I felt powerful, proud, and satisfied that I could help — for a brief moment. After a long silence, my woman, the one whom I was living with spoke in the soft tone she uses when she wants to remind me of just how far I am from the truth. Her words are stitched into my heart. She gently said, "Is that what our God of our fathers wants us to do, because I heard very different voice today at the village well?" She said, "I feel that he wants me to show her love, forgiveness, and extend mercy." Those were the last things I had on my mind at that time. The only thing I wanted her to do was to repay evil with more evil. The last thing I wanted to know in my anger was what God wanted her to do.

Though I was still upset for being her man who wasn't very helpful, I thought the best thing would be to stay calm, be quiet, and hit the pillow. So once again I stretched myself onto the bed and blew out the lamp for the last time and tried to sleep, to no avail. After a few moments laying there in the dark, something lit up within me. In my anger, I didn't want to let go of the water jar, just the way my woman had at the well wanted to make the rabbi pay for all the pain and evil her family and community had experienced at the hands of others. I felt the same anger.

But when an unnamed woman received kindness and truth from the rabbi, for the first time she could let go of the anger and hurt she had stuffed into the water jar and was ready to accept a new way of living. Leaving her water jar at the well symbolized that she was not going to continue reacting to evil deeds with evil actions, but rather, try to live a life of forgiveness, freedom, and peace.

Hearing those words from my woman and then feeling her go back to sleep, I knew this was anger from my own well of fear, shame, and hurt. This individual was only one reason that my anger surfaced. Now I had to deal with the root of the problem or it would lead me to places I never wanted to go. Today was the moment to let it go.

The first and second husbands stood there with me in silence, allowing God to fill us with his promised spring of living water that would wash away our past and our sins, and would extend forgiveness to us, others, and the community. For me, this was a moment of change, to be set free from my anger, forgiveness, and hatred, and be accepted — and from there to offer it to others. It was an unforgettable evening close to the well. I stood a while longer, attuned to this holy moment, breathing deep and allowing his invisible presence to wash me and set me free and set me on the right path of forgiveness and love.

Not Unlike Any of Them

After a while, I noticed the other three men near the left-behind water jar. They were standing together but individually dealing with their individual emotions, pain, and crises touched by the rabbi's words that day. This time I felt nudged to move closer to the third husband, the one who thought life's answers were found within his religion. Per him, he was practicing everything prescribed within his scriptures to fulfill his tradition. But he didn't realize how much his religion had oppressed many people and how much legality was choking life. Religion had become a lock rather than an illumination of God's goodness and grace.

That day the third husband was in a place where I once was, a place where religion had become a hindrance in extending grace to those who have been wronged. I knew very well how I had used religion as a cover to hide and condemn. I wanted to take the speck from my brother's eye when I had a log in my own. There was no mercy because I wasn't merciful to myself. I mourned as I thought of how my actions had prevented others from drinking from the well of living water.

Although the woman at the well refused to give Jesus a drink, he offered her more than a momentary quenching of thirst. When she accepted it, she let go of the water jar, she let go of the strong grip of religion and pain of legalism that she suffered at the hands of religious people. I realized that the freedom that Jesus offered helped both the third husband and me to step closer to the fountain, to that place of grace, freedom, and peace.

I recognized the fourth husband. His clothes and everything about him showed that he was a man in control, educated, and confident. Even though he projected unflappable poise, there was something missing. He was the last person I had expected to see standing there. The most appropriate place would have been for him to be addressing a large audience, talking about his latest discovery and how his research and work were helping people around the world. He had never exuded weakness or need, but right now in this moment I could feel that he had created his own easy answers to handle the sadness in his life through hard work and lots of achievements. But today, standing there, he was left with only questions to which he had no answers: *Why does evil happen in the world? Why did my children have to die a cruel death even before seeing the light of life? Why can't my wife and I have a normal relationship and a normal life?*

Further, he was confused about how to handle the pain, wondering, *how can I promise that there is a better world where there is no more pain? Are we humans always going to suffer and is this all life has to offer? Am I missing something? How long can we as a couple deny our feelings? Why must we go back to the same place every day to fill the water jar and too soon find that it's empty again?*

The fourth husband was standing there looking more confused and wanting to believe what he saw that day.

For the first time, he knew that there was no one truly greater than the one who spoke at the well that day. And oh, how he wanted to know the one who is the greatest and not settle for less. He was seeking the Savior, the Messiah who would rescue him from his fears and promise him something he had never experienced: the true hope.

My life had sometimes felt meaningless and hopeless wthout a relationship with God. I always thought that once I experienced him and once he came to me, then I would understand everything immediately and never want to leave him. But there were times that I ignored him and avoided him so he wouldn't open my eyes to my own foolishness. I was like this fourth husband who wanted to understand everything in a worldly way — rather than knowing this Savior in a personal, spiritual way. The Messiah had descended into our mess. The Almighty was talking to a woman at the well.

Ahni, the Sixth Man of Sychar

Standing alongside the first four husbands, I knew what I needed more than manufactured answers was the Savior himself, the Messiah. I needed the Son of God, who could set me free from myself. All my efforts and attempts to help myself fell short. Now I could see the one who came to empty himself to make me complete. I rejoiced, as did those standing with me. And this great Messiah was extending an invitation to become involved in his mission.

Of all the other men, the fifth husband was the one with whom I most closely identified. Most of his struggles are common to men everywhere. The lust of the eyes, pride of life, and the temptation of the flesh are the battles that most men fight and more often lose. The way most men are raised is to not admit our flaws and weaknesses. We do not want to expose our vulnerabilities to others, and we only face our true selves when we are caught and find no way to escape.

Our egos block us from seeking help and from seeing that our struggles are almost every man's. When men are together we can fight the battles well. We can be accountable to each other and deal with our shame, guilt, and anger. But that requires the risk of transparency. Our hiding entraps us further. But today was different, we were together.

The fifth husband's struggles were not new to me; I was facing the same demons daily and trying my best to put on a good face. I denied others access into my life. I became a person who gave less of himself to others and faced my pain and guilt alone in my tightly circumscribed space.

Even when I have tried to be religious or appear holy, I knew how much ungodliness still ran through me. I often cried alone, feeling the pangs of my hypocrisy; a man who shows himself to be in control but struggles to keep himself pure. I had often kept my heart closed so no conviction can walk through its door.

The fifth husband also did not deal with his heart. Therefore, he was stunted, chasing fantasies, shirking responsibilities, never growing into the man he was made to be.

A Tragic Cycle

Guilt and shame make for a tragic cycle, yet people make themselves quite comfortable with it. After trying to change and failing at it many times, they feel it is better not to try again. It's just easier to accept their failures as part of who they are.

The unnamed woman who tried to "fix" her men ended up with more trouble and pain. The only way she could change her life was honesty. She found her freedom in a redemptive encounter with rabbi Jesus at the well.

Ahni, the Sixth Man from Sychar

I saw the fifth husband for the first time stepping outside his own life and recognizing how his wife, who had been so close to him, had been under the spell of his manipulation. He saw how she was longing to be set free and once again live the dream she had for herself and for her future family. He understood now a new way of living. Determined, he moved closer to me. All I could offer him was a hug, an embrace to share the shame and guilt that we both felt. We stood in silence for some time and knew that we had to meet with the rabbi and experience him for ourselves — we had to be honest about our feelings and our fears. Together, as men, we could walk the path of freedom and see his light at the end of our dark tunnels.

All of us, I counted again, one, two, three, four, five, and, including me, six, made our way slowly toward the path that led to the town to meet with the Seventh Man. The path was dark, as it was now nighttime, and it was empty save for us. Yet we didn't fear because we were together. We understood each other's silence, our struggles, our aches, and our wonderings. We wanted to be together because we were all broken in our own way: we had failed, but finally, now there was hope.

We saw lights shining at a distance from the town of Sychar. We knew we were on the right path, and at that moment we were filled with tremendous joy and hope. Our hope came from the one who loved us above all else; he loved us so much that he approached a hopeless woman at the well who then led us all to him. And all of us held a common thread, a connection to her life and our own sin. He accepted her, forgave her, and she was changed from within. And through her a new fountain of sparkling, fresh, living water was flowing through the lives of the people from Sychar. And we all felt that thirst deep within us.

I walked along with the five other men from Sychar. Together we knew we needed help and we needed someone greater than Jacob and ourselves. We needed the Savior. The one who was here to meet with us and the one willing to take us beyond the well. As we made our entrance through the gate of Sychar, there was a strange sense of stillness, something rising within all of us and together we wanted to experience it. One step at a time.

James Levi

Chapter 8

Well to Spring

"Many of the Samaritans from that town believed in Him because of the woman's testimony: "He told me everything I ever did." So, when the Samaritans came to him, they urged him to stay with them, and he stayed two days. And because of his words many more became believers." (John 4:39-41).

Rabbi Jesus was in Sychar for two days, and the people from Samaria wanted him to stay longer. This had never happened before — a Jewish rabbi was never invited into the homes of Samaritan people. The Jews and Samaritans kept each other at a distance. But today that relationship changed because an unnamed woman accepted the offer to drink water from a different source. Rather than drinking from the well that could run dry, she chose to drink living water from the fountain of life.

She was an outcast, expelled from the community by those who were also hurting. When no one from within the community stepped forward to show her any compassion, a man made a holy interruption of her noontime schedule to speak with her, even though he was not one of her people. He didn't avoid her because of her past, but he instead accepted her for who she was: a child of God. He came to show her that she was above everything that had ever happened to her in her life. Her life was more precious than all the failures and mistakes that she had committed.

She wanted to live life beyond the well.

The stranger sitting at the well met her there with a promise.

> Even now the one who reaps draws a wage and harvests a crop for eternal life, so that the sower and the reaper may be glad together. Thus, the saying 'One sows, and another reaps' is true. I sent you to reap what you have not worked for. Others have done the hard work, and you have reaped the benefits of their labor" (John 4:36-38).

When she told the villagers about the man at the well, she was working for God Almighty, bringing in a harvest for his kingdom. All her previous men and the others came to hear what he had to say and became believers. None of her religious activities of the past or prayers had ever made any difference. But the man she met that day was greater than Jacob (who had given the well to her people), and he was even greater than all the prophets she had ever known. The one she had denied water was the one willing to die for her — and for all of humanity. The one whom she avoided because of her own issues gave her the   living water, though it would cost him his life. After she understood this truth, her life was never the same.

She was no longer afraid of letting people into her life. Before, her past experiences and the way people treated her dictated how she responded. She was caged in her past and was also caged in her future because of her fears.

But today the meeting with the rabbi Jesus changed her and allowed her to live a bigger, expanded life. She was not going to be ruled by fear and rejection. She would not give up on people because of how they might deal with her and treat her. She decided that her reactions toward others would be based on how the rabbi dealt with her. Despite her treating him harshly, he was kind and extended his grace and mercy, which spoke to the center of her being. Yes, there would be times when she would again be rejected, and, yes, there would be people who would try again to abuse her — but she saw a new option available, a new perspective dawned on her, a new scope of her ministry widened. She decided that she wanted to live a life filled with hope, faith, and trust.

She was now willing to allow people to come into her life once again; there would be no more living a life of shame and fear. She was not going to accept the monotonous life of going to and from the well, hiding and always on the lookout for people who might hurt or judge her. No, now she wanted to live a life focused on what God thought about her and what he wanted from her. She came to realize that her life was much more than she or others had made it to be, she knew it belonged to God and it was worth sharing for his glory.

She wasn't going to live in embarrassment anymore; rather, she would embrace the gift of God and walk in abundant life. It was a great relief to feel this freedom and be unburdened. This was *life beyond the well;* it was life springing forth from the fountain of living water.

She wanted her people to experience what she had experienced. Life at the well was all about *her* and what *she* got and how *she* survived in an abusive community. The negative experiences in her life constrained who she was and who she could be. Life at the well was about self-preservation and making meaning within that narrow space rather than living a freer, richer, fuller life with others and for others.

But this day, she was ready to move beyond herself and was willing to think about the good news and share it with the people in her community, those who were going through similar pain and suffering. Her life was enlarged with just one encounter with rabbi Jesus, who came to live for others. He came not to be served but to serve. She adopted that same spirit.

Living beyond the well-meant inviting the community to participate in the truth she had experienced. Never had she been concerned about the needs and feelings of other people, but she would not focus on herself anymore. She would now live for her people and for all who were needy and hurting.

Moving beyond the well was the first symbolic step toward welcoming truth — though it was uncomfortable and sometimes painful. For a long time, hating the Jews had closed her off. She now allowed God to speak into her life and there was breakthrough. Today, she was able to see that the truth was bigger than what a community can contain. *Salvation is from the Jews and she accepted that; worship was beyond location and she recognized that; the Messiah had already come, and she received that.* The pain of the past and hurt of the present had prohibited the truth from being recognized by her people.

No more closed doors, no more unwelcome signs; the truth of God was now being embraced. Moving from the well-meant dropping the water jar of the religious traditions blocking her from the truth that God revealed.

Meeting the rabbi, the one who knew everything about her, gave the unnamed woman boldness to be open to receive healing, and in turn she became an inspiration for others to be open and vulnerable to receive healing. The well was no longer a place where she went to keep things hidden deep inside. Now she wanted to tell the people how a hidden life can be full of chaos, anger, and trouble. But when opened by grace by the rabbi's hands, and when mercy and love are extended, then each person in the community can find lasting peace, health, and hope.

****

This story began with an unnamed, ordinary, and damaged woman, but she was just part of a larger story, of a community and the baggage that was hidden underneath. Each of us has baggage that we carry, due to our environment, our past, and by virtue of just being human. Like the unnamed woman and each of her husbands, all human beings deal with their baggage in their own way and try to convince themselves and the world that everything is all right — when deep within we know nothing is.

That day the way Rabbi Jesus Christ dealt with the woman is the same how He deals with us in a very powerful yet gentle way. The communal healing began by travelling a different route, taking risks, and meeting people on a different side. Reaching out to a woman in a very vulnerable position opened her up to him and, in the process, allowed him to touch her community and her world.

James Levi

Chapter 9

The Seventh Man

> They said to the woman, "We no longer believe just because of what you said; now we have heard for ourselves, and we know that this man really is the Savior of the world" (John 4:42).

A stranger came to Sychar at noon and said, "I thirst." He was in need, vulnerable, and appeared weak. What was the thirst that this rabbi Jesus expressed in Sychar? We see him again shouting it out at the top of his lungs: "I thirst!" from the cross of Calvary when he was about to die, hanging between two criminals. Who is this man who comes asking for a drink from an ordinary person and then promises the extraordinary fountain of living water?

Some refused to give him drink, and some still refuse to come to him, some called him a liar filled with demons, and some cast him out of their synagogues and their towns. Yet a few stayed with him and a few offered him a cup of cold water and many still came to him. Crowds thronged but each person had a personal story, a story in common with the unnamed woman as well as the five men who walked away from the well that evening and then spent two glorious days with the rabbi. They, like many others, followed him and his teachings for the rest of their lives.

******

I, Ahni, the sixth man from Sychar, also have a story of meeting this rabbi as did those five men. They exposed that which was hidden in me, that which was kept in secret.

My Story

I would have never gone to meet the rabbi had he come to my town as a weak, needy, and thirsty person. That's because for many years, I looked at God as all-powerful, self-sufficient, and in control. Eventually, I came to realize that my point of view had been conditioned by my culture and the people with whom I was raised. I didn't realize that God's thirst was much deeper. His thirst was, and is, to fill his children with living water that gives them meaning, purpose, and life.

I grew up with poor self-image and I didn't think people liked me. So, from a very young age I wanted to be someone else. Everything I did was to please others. My very identity and self-worth were derived from other people's criticism or praise.

When people can't recognize or acknowledge the intrinsic value that they are created with, they will often settle for something less and try to find value in that. Soon they will find that the life they are living is empty and meaningless. I lived such a life and, to be honest, I still do sometimes. I want to be accepted and liked by others, but that pursuit is never-ending because there is nothing that I can do that can completely and fully satisfy others.

The problem with living someone else's life is that every day you wake up confused, unsure of who you are. Daily, you lose even more of your sense of self, which can be one of the greatest human tragedies. It prevents you from becoming everything that God intended *you* to be, your life is not your own, and you are as good as being dead. Because of those dead feelings we often bring more death upon ourselves as we indulge in negative activities that cause fear and anger.

I became such a person. I was full of negativity and quick to criticize others because I was hurting inside and full of self-doubt. I wanted to cause doubt in others' lives, too. This cycle eventually seemed normal for me because I became a master at faking it and making up what were fundamentally lies and living with hypocrisy. Eventually I came to believe that I could never actually live who I truly was. I was ashamed of myself and when others saw I wasn't authentic, I become angry. I was trying to do it my way and not the way God wanted.

Then Came the Lady

Then life changed. I met the rabbi. Not literally, but through my woman, the one I was living with. We have been together as a couple, but she never wanted to commit to the relationship as she had been hurt in her past associations with other men. She was married five times before but that didn't bother me as I was not ready for any commitment. We lived our lives hoping we will be able to make it work. She didn't believe anymore in the institution of marriage because she was hurt, betrayed and abused in all the relationship and I, Ahni wasn't a man who was willing to make any commitment. I believed in keeping my options opened as well as reap all the benefits that I can gain. But such loose living together lifestyle wasn't helping us, rather it was creating more pain which we would just slip it under the carpet. We both though living together yet were drifting apart many miles away from each other.

But then things changed.

It happened one day.

My woman as usual had gone to the well, the place where she would often go to have some peace, sanity and space from all that was going on in her and our world.

But that day everything changed. She met a man. She met the Rabbi. She came back as a different person. I knew she was born-again. Every moment since then have been living with a saint. There was no more of that old self of hatred, anger, jealousy, they all vanished, and I was astounded. She introduced me to a life that was more like Jesus intended. She didn't come with all the answers, nor did she come to change me, but she came like the rabbi came in her brokenness. She came to me in weakness and was vulnerable and asked me for a drink, asked for help and admitted her need. She was thirsty to show me the love of Christ.

I would fake, I would act, and I would never admit my fears and shortcomings. But as I witnessed the life she lived, I began to consider the life of the one who had influenced her. I looked closely and found that the same rabbi Jesus that had entered the life of the unnamed woman at the well had come into her life, too. As I learned more about him, I was, for the first time, unashamed to be me. It was safe to be weak, broken, and hurt. I cried, but it was all OK.

Together we sat with the master and asked him to meet us at the well, just as she had brought her fellow villagers to the well. All the things I had been running after thinking they would fill my life never did and they were all meaningless. But what I saw in my woman's life was joy and peace and healing. Through her love of Jesus, I experienced forgiveness, acceptance, and hope.

I was a new person. I no longer lived with low self-esteem. I didn't have to put down other people when they were mean. I didn't have to falsely exaggerate and disingenuously praise others to be aggrandized in return. I could accept myself the way I was because someone had showed me love, acceptance, and forgiveness, just as he had done for the woman at the well. I, too, had received his wonderful gift of God's grace. He met me at my own well, the place where I would hide my fears and struggles. Finally, I understood what he meant when he said he was thirsty. He was inviting me to give up my shame and pain. He was asking me to open my heart and let go of my water jar and live a life of abundance, grace, and to drink of the spring of living water that only he can give.

I do not say that I have attained it all or arrived at my destination, but I know I am on the right journey with people like Aleph, Beit, Gimel, Dalet, and Hei, and together we can walk toward our healing and to a life of hope.

The only thing Jesus requires is for us to come to him, thirsty for the living water he offers to all who ask.

*****

The left behind book and the man from the Island

A lot have changed since Jay and me had that mystical encounter with Ahni. We knew our lives were going to be changed. As I poured over the pages of the book left behind, I was experiencing powerful transformation within my soul. As every word was affecting my spirit, emotion and my life. Many of the issues from my past that were carefully and deeply hidden within started to be surfacing and to be honest I didn't know how to deal with it. I was confused and for many days and even some sleepless nights. I wanted to blame Jay for stopping the car at the first place and giving the lift to a stranger on a deserted highway. I got angry with Ahni and the frustrated with the book he left behind that had caused so much untold misery within my spirit. I could very well identify myself with the woman at the well, who was going through the turmoil within her soul. During one of those intense painful nights, I cried out to the one who came to meet the woman in her brokenness and struggle to set her free. And it did happen. I don't know how long I stayed late that evening, but I knew I wasn't alone. I started pouring out my heart and I knew he was able to take it all and was there to hold me in his embrace. I felt that assurance that he was going to walk with me. As I stood up to walk back to my home, I could see the sun rising gently and shining its bright rays into the dark sky. I knew I was filled. I knew there was a spring of living water making its presence deep within me. I knew I didn't have to go back to some of the old places, my wells and I could live this life in the newness and the power of the one who came to meet me in the middle of the night. Next many days were spent carefully translating the book for the people to read who would not be able to have the benefit of knowing the language. I started sharing with everyone about the book. I started teaching about the concepts that each of the Samaritan woman's husband represented and many of us struggle with and the seventh man who came to heal, restore and give a new life to each of us. I was amazed at the stories that I was hearing about the affects these six men's as well as the woman's life was making on the ordinary but messed up, normal yet broken people all over. I didn't know how I can thank Ahni for the incredible gift that he had left behind for us that day. As more and more people were reading hearing about those stories and sharing about their own struggles, pain and addictions, I saw what Ahni did was creating many communities of broken people who could come to the well and get healed. Though I was very glad to hear about the impact and the imprint the book was making, I also didn't want some people to be left behind because they could get an opportunity to hear about these amazing encounter of these people of Sychar and the people I came in contact or those who were able to get access to the book. Therefore, I decided I should also go like the Samaritan woman and tell everyone about the Messiah who has come into the world.

A few years ago, I was travelling overseas into the ancient world, some of the places where those people who had initially heard the woman had lived and their lives had impacted countless others there. On this particular day, I was travelling to an Island and the boat was filled to the capacity with young and old, rich and poor and all kinds of people. But I knew deep down that none of them have ever heard about the man one of their ancestors had met and how her life had changed and affected many from her village. I was sad and also tired because of the journey. I decided to go down into the lower part of the deck and rest. I always carried the book with me that Ahni had left behind. I kept it close to my head and slept off. After some time, when I woke up, I saw one of the crewmen came over and sat next to me. We started talking and over the next hour he shared all about his life, his world and his work as a crewman taking people to and from different Islands. As I was headed to the last Island, there weren't many passengers and as I got to know this young man, I was surprised to know that his native language was the same as the one that the book was written in. Though I was surprised it was hard for me to believe it that he had never heard the woman that was mentioned in the book. As our time to disembark came, I could sense a deep urge from within me to give this book to the young man who needed more than anyone else. He had shared some of the difficulties he was going through among some of the rough workers on the boat. He was very grateful and excited about the book he received from me as a gift. I could see him holding it much reverence and piety. As I stepped away from the dock, I could see him slowly walking away from me and returning to the same bench we were sitting and opening the book with a much anticipation and thirst. I was glad I left the book that was handed to me by Ahni to the next man. As I walked away, I felt the same warmth, the Samaritan woman felt that day seeing a large crowd coming to the Messiah and sitting close to him and enjoying his presence. She knew deep within her spirit the feeling of birthing of a spring of living water welling up to eternal life. I couldn't agree more.

Who Is Thirsty?

> Jesus answered, "Everyone who drinks this water will be
> thirsty again, but whoever drinks the water I give them will
> never thirst. Indeed, the water I give them will become in
> them a spring of water welling up to eternal life." The
> woman said to him, "Sir, give me this water so that I won't
> get thirsty and have to keep coming here to draw water."
> (John 4:13-15)

Is the spring of water flowing from us living or are our
springs polluted, not just useless but also harmful? Are we
aware of our thirst today or are we only thinking we are filled?
Maybe we are unaware of our thirst after being religious for so
many years. Have we covered up our pain and do we ignore
others? If so, let's come to him and allow him to make us
thirsty for him. May Christ fill us with his living water so that
we may no longer thirst again and hurt others.

Sometime later, before this Seventh Man breathed his last
and gave up his spirit, he cried out: *"I am thirsty,"* It is an
invitation to all today who are hiding, heaving, and hurting to
come to him and drink the very same water he offered the
woman and all the villagers at the well. It is water for our souls,
water for our world and water that is the only river whose
course leads us into eternity.

About the Author

James Levi is a Christian minister who served with the Texas Department of Criminal Justice in the United States. He is a graduate of Fuller Theological Seminary. His Ph.D. is in international development with a specialization in Christian leadership.

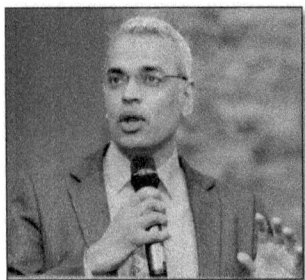

Dr. Levi was born and raised in India. After completing his master's degree in biochemistry, he worked in the healthcare industry. Later, he felt called to pursue graduate studies in the United States, giving him the added advantage of skillfully working cross-culturally with people in various international contexts. He is married and they have two beautiful daughters. He is also a licensed private pilot who enjoys time with his family.

In addition to *The Seventh Man*, he is the author of *38 at Estelle, The Living Clay, Visible Faith* and *Higher Ground.*

*9 7 8 1 7 3 4 4 5 5 1 2 0 *